Liberty of Conscience and the Growth of

Religious Diversity in Early America, 1636–1786

Sponsored by

The Lilly Endowment, Inc.

The Rhode Island Committee for the Humanities

The Rhode Island Heritage Commission

Rhode Island 350

The Rhode Island Council of Churches

The Loeb Foundation

Liberty of Conscience and the Growth of

Religious Diversity in Early America, 1636–1786

by Carla Gardina Pestana

with a foreword by Martin E. Marty

The John Carter Brown Library

Providence, Rhode Island

1986

This catalogue has been published in honor of the 350th
anniversary of the founding of the state of Rhode Island.

The John Carter Brown Library is an institution for
advanced research in the humanities at Brown University.

ISBN 0-916617-02-5

To my parents

Contents

Illustrations

Foreword

It is almost certain that never in history have more religious groups coexisted within a nation than do in the United States. It is equally almost certain that never have there been so many assurances of religious freedom as in the United States.

The two, "religious diversity" and "liberty of conscience," obviously connect. Voltaire had observed concerning England what almost became a principle in the United States: "If there were one religion...its despotism would be terrible; if there were only two, they would destroy each other; but there are thirty, and therefore they live in peace and happiness." James Madison seconded this: "In a free government the security for civil rights must be the same as that for religious rights; it consists in one case in the multiplicity of interests and in the other the multiplicity of sects."

Mere diversity does not assure "liberty of conscience." As I write, modern Lebanon and a host of other nations have diversity without a polity. The United States somehow found a means to forge a nation with some common purpose among individuals and groups who did not share ultimate concern in respect to their philosophy and ways of life, their faiths.

The United States "somehow" found a means. That "somehow" is the subject of this catalogue and the exhibit it represents. One may speak of the events that produced "liberty of conscience" or, better, liberty for expression of conscience, as a revolution. Two features of revolution make it hard to understand this one. First, after they are over, it is hard to conceive how life had been before. Second, we are schooled to think of shots being fired, of bloodshed, in revolution. Both conventional ways of thinking call for some examination.

As for the difficulty people have conceiving of what life was like before revolution, the drastic change in colonial American life as the United States was being formed is a good case in point. It is hard to convince latter-day Americans that most of their colonial foreparents came not to assure religious freedom in general but only to seek it for themselves. Many of them were ready to set up little empires that united church and state at least as firmly as had any in Europe. When we hear that religious freedom is suppressed in authoritarian societies on the Right and the Left, this seems like a novelty. Yet it had been the normal state of affairs almost everywhere for many centuries. The first signals of "toleration" had begun to come in England and elsewhere, but religious freedom that assured rights to non-believers as well as to all sorts of believers awaited a revolution.

Second, we think of revolutions as using cannon and bombs, but this one did not. It occurred during the American War of Independence, a revolution that did produce bloodshed, and so the quiet revolution in church and state has been obscured. There are no dead bodies on this landscape. Some dissenters and fighters for freedom were jailed, to be sure. Madison spoke of a "diabolical, hell-conceived principle" that left some ministers of the Gospel behind bars.

His observation of the terrible workings of that principle led him to urge that "the right of every man is to liberty—not toleration." The First Amendment to the United States Constitution expressed something of the revolution in understandings. If the American Revolution left landmarks—Bunker Hill and Fort Ticonderoga and Yorktown, with monuments and memorials still to be seen—the revolution that assured liberty of conscience in matters of religion left less obvious ones.

This exhibit brings together some of the traces, chiefly in documentary form, of the move across the colonies to produce the most drastic change in church-state polity in fourteen-hundred years. In the fourth century, Christians came to dominate the Roman Empire and to establish their faith at the expense of others. Even the Protestant Reformation of the sixteenth century did little to change the pattern; most of the reformers who were "winners" established their version of the church and pursued dissenters. Change came "somehow" in Rhode Island, Pennsylvania, Virginia, and then across the colonies and in the new United States.

That "somehow" can look like luck; Voltaire was really describing how religiously diverse nations can luck out. It can seem to be based on mere expediency: it was practical for Americans to push religion from the center of the stage politically and allow themselves to be productive without distraction. Some see it as ideology: people of the Enlightenment or of fierce religious convictions fought for freedom. The documents here suggest that the revolution for religious freedom included these elements and more.

What is surprising is to see how diverse were the interests of those who advocated and produced change. We see angry pamphlets by semi-literate farmers and eloquent documents from Virginia country estates; there are highly personal prophecies and calculated political proposals. What becomes clear is that no single individual is responsible for the polity that James Madison, Thomas Jefferson, and other founders gave voice to. No single religion or non-religion by itself could have produced the liberty that went beyond toleration. The general notion that a nation could exist without an official religion to bind it spread across the colonies. It was expressed in print that can be found in archives of states and in church towers alike. This exhibit offers a rich sample of the argument and artifact. It exists to inform. It may also lead citizens of a later day to ponder what life would have been like without this revolution, and to resolve that liberty of conscience continue to be insured. Madison put it well: "It is proper to take alarm at the first experiment on our liberties. We hold this prudent jealousy to be the first duty of citizens." This catalogue depicts something of that prudent jealousy which, instead of being mere self-interest, could then and now remain "one of the noblest characteristics" of this people.

Martin E. Marty
The University of Chicago

14

Preface

It is not now fashionable among historians as it once was to write the history of the United States as the progressive and almost inevitable unfolding of human liberty over the course of three centuries. Such thematic treatments, by making the past appear pre-determined, tend to minimize the real crises of decision, the passionate struggles and even martyrdoms that men and women underwent for matters of faith, with no certainty about the outcome.

Yet even free choices and deep struggles within individual souls are influenced by circumstances, and in the area of religion in American history the circumstances seem to have strongly favored liberty. In the case of the great foreshadower of American religious liberty, Roger Williams, individual decision and historical circumstances came together just right. Williams's prescient vision of the secular and neutral state, which led to the founding of Rhode Island as the first government in modern history that expressly rejected civil coercion of religious belief, made good sense in America.

Hence, the position taken by Thomas Jefferson on church and state relations 150 years later appears to be the culmination of a logical and irresistible development that began with Williams, although Williams and Jefferson had vastly different motives. Historical circumstances in British America eventually predisposed men toward accepting the equality of all beliefs and the detachment of the state from involvement not only with any particular religion but with religion itself. As James Madison said, the passage by the Virginia Assembly in 1786 of Jefferson's bill for "Religious Freedom" had "in this Country extinguished forever the ambitious hope of making laws for the human mind."

This catalogue is rich in historical detail and example, but it wisely does not attempt to plumb the miracle of how it came to be that Americans in the British colonies escaped potential bloodbaths in the name of religion. Suffering and persecution there were, but relatively little compared to the power for violent confrontation that religious belief is capable of generating, as has been demonstrated to the present-day in Ireland, Lebanon, and other places.

Instead of trying to explain, Carla Pestana's narrative celebrates the numerous accommodations that went along with the growing diversity of sectarian opinion in early America, beginning with the original hero, Roger Williams.

It is no accident, of course, that in 1986 the John Carter Brown Library has mounted a major exhibition on the theme of religious liberty. Exactly three hundred and fifty years earlier, Roger Williams had fled the Massachusetts Bay Colony, where he had become persona non grata, and founded the colony that was to become the state of Rhode Island. It seemed to the staff of the Library that this anniversary deserved some attention and celebration, not just because Rhode Island was founded but because of *how* it was founded, with the open hand of peace rather than the fist of coercion.

Nearly all of the materials in this exhibition are from the John Carter Brown Library collection (the few exceptions are noted in the catalogue and on the exhibition labels). The story of the Library's strength in colonial American religion begins with Harold Brown (1863-1900), one of John Carter Brown's two sons, who, like his father (and his brother, John Nicholas), was a serious book collector. What is notable about Harold Brown in relation to this exhibition is that he took a special interest in the general theme of what he called "the Church in America" and bought for the Library hundreds of religious tracts and sermons that compose the core of this exhibition. Many of these items could not be bought today at any price, since the few copies that have survived are all now in institutional collections and will never again appear on the market. In the eighty-six years since Harold Brown's death, various librarians and curators at the Library have continued to strengthen the Library's holdings of printed materials in the area of colonial American religion, with the result that the Library now has one of the finest such collections in the world.

It has been said that the Protestant Reformation could not have succeeded to the degree that it did had not the invention of printing with movable metal type occurred approximately sixty years earlier, in the mid-fifteenth century. Luther and his successors were able to use print to attract support, and for the next two hundred years most of the printing that took place in Europe and America pertained directly to religion. Polemics, liturgies, catechisms, psalms, testaments, apologies, spiritual accounts, hagiography, and many other types of religious literature poured forth from all the presses, Protestant and Catholic. In the British-American colonies, printing began in 1640 and was heavily religious in nature until the mid-eighteenth century. The history of religion and the history of printing, in short, are closely allied in this period, and in this exhibition, aside from its substantive content, a full range of religious printing is illustrated, from the crude woodcuts of the Boston imprint *The History of the Holy Jesus* (1746) to the sophistication of a London *Book of Common Prayer* (1662) published on the occasion of the restoration of the Stuarts to the English throne.

For readers with a particular interest in historical and descriptive bibliography and the history of religious printing, the Library has published separately a technical *Bibliographical Supplement* to this exhibition catalogue, which may be purchased for $10.00 by writing directly to the Library. The research, writing, and typing of the *Supplement* was undertaken by Mrs. Helena Costa. Mrs. Costa is one of several Library staff members who contributed to this project on "Liberty of Conscience and the Growth of Religious Diversity in Early America." Acknowledgment by the author of this assistance appears at the end of the catalogue. Particular mention must be made here, however, of the help of a non-staff member, Elizabeth Lilla, who served as copy editor and proofreader of the catalogue and the *Supplement*.

The publication of this catalogue, the research behind it, and the mounting of the exhibition at the Library would not have been possible without the financial support of several outside agencies. A grant early in 1985 by the Rhode Island Committee for the Humanities enabled the research for the project to begin. This was followed in the summer by a major grant from the Lilly Endowment of Indiana, which has underwritten not only much of the specific work represented here but also the ongoing cataloguing, according to the highest bibliographical standards, of hundreds of eighteenth-century American religious imprints in the Library's collection. This cataloguing data will be entered into the Research Libraries Information Network and thus be made available to many other librarians and individual scholars around the country. I wish to express the gratitude of the John Carter Brown Library for this essential grant support.

One of the Library's goals in the preparation of this catalogue has been the publication of a work that would provide historical perspective on an issue that continues to be a source of friction in American society, namely church and state relations. To that end, of the 1,200 copies of this work that have been printed, the Library has given away approximately 300 to public, school, and college libraries in Rhode Island.

Norman Fiering
Director and Librarian
The John Carter Brown Library

CHAPTER I

The Insistence on Religious Uniformity

By the last decades of the eighteenth century the United States encompassed peoples of many different faiths. Some had brought their beliefs with them to the British North American colonies, while others had converted to, or even created, new faiths once in the New World. The religious diversity of the new nation was one of its most remarkable features. In a sermon preached in 1783 Congregational minister and Yale president Ezra Stiles predicted that the United States would soon include every Christian sect. Furthermore, he was pleased to add, each of these sects would be granted the freedom to worship in its own way.

The religious diversity Stiles described and the liberty of conscience he praised went hand in hand. For one thing, the right of liberty of conscience made it possible for people with diverse beliefs to join together in founding a new nation. Without such a right, political agreement would have been much harder to achieve, since each sect or denomination would have feared possible domination by every other. In addition, this novel experiment in republican government depended upon freedom of opinion. The human mind had to be free to choose in matters of faith as well as in matters of politics if the experiment were to succeed.

The predictions made by Stiles have been borne out in the last two centuries. To this day the citizens of the United States worship in many different ways, and this freedom of belief and worship is something we enjoy and have come to expect. The separation of church and state, which prevents the state from exercising power in the realm of religion, has become one of the cardinal tenets of this nation.

Such freedom in faith and worship and such detachment on the part of the state are relatively new concepts. Both the religious diversity and the liberty of conscience that flourish in the United States today, with no one denomination favored by the government, would have been abhorrent to the founders of the first English colonies. The vast majority of the English believed that conformity in religion was not only required by God, but was politically and socially necessary. Every European nation had an established church, and all but the Dutch republic persecuted anyone who dissented from the established faith. Catholics and Protestants were in complete agreement that uncontrolled religious diversity was disruptive, causing people of different faiths to fight among themselves and to dishonor truth. Complete religious liberty, it was said, encouraged the unguided individual to wander off into heretical, bizarre, seditious, licentious behavior. Thus, the first English colonies—Virginia, Plimouth Plantation, and the Massachusetts Bay Colony—were all founded with the assumption that religious uniformity would be a major attribute of each settlement. The most a dissenter in one of these colonies could expect would be a watchful indulgence of his differences; there was always the possibility of severe persecution.

Over the course of the seventeenth century the religious composition of the English colonies changed drastically. In some places unchecked diversity developed despite the best efforts of the authorities. This was so with Virginia and Massachusetts, as we shall see. In other colonies religious heterogeneity was the unintended result of policies aimed at attracting settlers or at providing a refuge for a single group. The latter was the case in the "Catholic" colony of Maryland, where Roman Catholics were able to worship only because the laws relating to religion were so vaguely worded as to permit all forms of Christianity. Finally, in a few very unusual cases, religious uniformity was never even sought after, and different sects were accorded equal treatment. In 1636 this radical experiment in "soul liberty" set the tiny colony of Rhode Island apart from nearly all the rest of the European world, winning "Rogue's Island" an unsavory reputation among the advocates of religious conformity. Beginning in the 1670s and 1680s, the Quakers who controlled the colonies of West Jersey and Pennsylvania also granted liberty of conscience to all inhabitants.

During the colonial period the religious heterodoxy that developed—despite all efforts to suppress nonconformity—helped to undermine the belief that government control over religious beliefs and practices was a necessary component of a harmonious society. At this time many colonists came to consider the right of the individual to choose freely in such matters more important, and even more expedient, than coerced conformity. This transformation in religious attitudes and practices was truly remarkable. It was certainly one of the most significant unforeseen consequences of the British colonization of North America, and it came to shape the new nation. The struggle of various peoples to worship freely culminated in the constitutional guarantee of freedom of worship for all and in the detachment of the civil state from the spiritual realm. Thus, in early America the growth of religious diversity and the acceptance of the right to liberty of conscience went hand in hand.

Anglicanism in Virginia

Virginia, founded in 1607, was the first successful English colony. The official church in Virginia was the Church of England, and residents of the colony were taxed to support the Church, just as they had been in England. The Anglican church had been created during the reign of Henry VIII, almost seventy-five years earlier. Henry had severed England's ties with the Roman Catholic Church, creating an English church with the monarch at its head. The Anglican Church retained a measure of the doctrine, ritual, and hierarchical organization of the Catholic Church, making it one of the more conservative churches to arise out of the Protestant Reformation. Queen Elizabeth, whose reign ended four years before Virginia was settled, had worked to systematize this national church. Under her direction the Church adopted Thirty-nine Articles of Religion, which outlined the tenets of faith, and a revised Book of Common Prayer, which provided the liturgy for the church services (figure I.1.).

As a matter of course, Virginia (named for the Virgin Queen) was an Anglican colony, and Holy Communion was celebrated immediately upon the first settlers' arrival. The colony's backers agreed on the importance of spreading the Anglican faith to the New World, both by establishing the Church in the colony and by working to convert the native people of the area. In fact, among the English supporters of the initial colonization effort were a number of Anglican bishops and other clergy. Eventually, ministers who came to Virginia were required to take an oath of conformity to the Church of England.

The colony's early years were troubled. Many of the first settlers died, and the company that had been organized to oversee the affairs of the colony collapsed in bankruptcy. Reorganization of the colony under royal control in

1
Church of England.
Book of Common Prayer and
Administration of the Sacraments.
(London, 1662)

Originally compiled during the brief reign
of Edward VI (1547–1553) and later revised
under Elizabeth, the Book of Common
Prayer contained the liturgy used by the
Church of England. It was often beautifully
printed and sumptuously illustrated, and
was reprinted many times over the years.
This edition was the first to be published
after the Church of England was reestab-
lished with the Restoration of the Stuart
monarchy in 1660 (See chapter III, below,
and figure I.1.).

2
William Crashaw (1572–1626).
A Sermon Preached in London before the
Right Honourable the Lord Lawarre, Lord
Governour and Captaine Generall of
Virginea.
(London, 1610)

This sermon by an Anglican clergyman was
delivered before the governor and many of
the backers of the colony of Virginia at a
time when the colony was just three years
old and floundering badly. The Reverend
Crashaw, had an explanation for this discouraging state of affairs, however. The
devil, he said, opposed the colonization of
Virginia because he wanted to keep the
natives ignorant of Christianity. If the colony was successful, the Indians would be
converted to the Church of England, and
Satan would lose these heathen souls. According to Crashaw's reasoning, the colony's initial failure merely proved that the
project was worthwhile, and he counseled
his listeners to renew their efforts on behalf of this important cause. In later years
it seemed the devil *was* thwarted and Virginia securely planted–although full-scale
missionary efforts and mass conversion of
the local tribes did not follow.

I.1. Charles I, sympathetically
portrayed in an edition of the
Book of Common Prayer (London, 1662). After the English
Civil War and the reign of
Oliver Cromwell and his son,
the Stuart family was returned
to the throne of England. With
this Restoration, the Church of
England regained its place as
the national religion. A new
edition of the *Book of Common
Prayer* was issued shortly
thereafter. Concern about
reasserting the royal family's
legitimacy was revealed in this
engraving, which depicted the
executed king as a martyr to
God's cause.

3
William Strachey (1572?–1621).
For the Colony in Virginea Britania: Lawes Divine, Morall and Martiall.
(London, 1612)

The laws governing the five-year-old colony of Virginia were published in this 1612 pamphlet. Blasphemy, speaking against the Trinity, and any act that was found to be disrespectful of God were punishable by the death penalty. Less severe penalties were meted out to Sabbath-breakers, people who failed to attend church ser-vices, and those who committed sacrilege. These laws indicated the government's willingness to punish religious offenders. The large number of laws relating to matters of faith and the severity of the punishments for those who broke them were typical of this era in which religious conformity was still considered a necessary component of civil peace.

4
Hugh Jones (ca. 1670–1760).
The Present State of Virginia.
(London, 1724)

Pamphleteers frequently published reports on the situation in the various colonies for the interested English reader. In this work, Hugh Jones described early eighteenth-century Virginia. Although the Church of England was the official religion in both Virginia and England, Jones had to explain the vestry system used in the colony to his English audiences.

1624 strengthened England's commitment to make Virginia an Anglican settlement, but the plan to transplant the Church of England as an effective and all-pervasive religious institution was one thing; implementing such a plan turned out to be quite a different matter.

Many of the problems the Anglican establishment faced in the New World resulted from the great distance that separated the colony from the Church in England. Because of this obstacle, the Anglican Church always had trouble ministering to the English inhabitants of Virginia. Once the colony was firmly established it was divided into parishes patterned after the English system, each parish to be staffed by an ordained minister. But the colony continually suffered from a shortage of clergymen. English ministers were not easily attracted to Virginia, and for many years the educational facilities needed for training them in the colony simply did not exist. Even after the College of William and Mary was founded, in part to address this problem, it was necessary for ministerial candidates to travel to London to be ordained. The Church considered sending a bishop who would be resident in the American colonies—an arrangement that would have alleviated this aspect of the problem—but this idea was never acted on.

Even if each parish had been adequately staffed, the plantation economy that developed in the southern colonies encouraged geographic dispersion of the settlers. The parishes were huge, and many people could not, or did not choose to, travel great distances to church on Sunday. Particularly in frontier communities, many colonists were completely "unchurched." These people would prove receptive to the evangelical ministers of other faiths who would travel through the southern back country in later years. Despite inroads made by other religious groups, Anglicanism remained the established faith in Virginia until the American Revolution. Other faiths might be nominally tolerated, but the state placed restrictions on them and tried to control their presence and prevent their growth.

In response to these discouraging circumstances, a number of innovations developed in colonial Anglicanism. For example, in the absence of a qualified minister, a lay person was chosen to read the church service on the Sabbath.

WILLIAM the Third, By the Grace of God, of England, Scotland, France, and Ireland, King, Defender of the Faith, &c. To all Christian People, to whom these Presents shall come, Greeting:

I. Whereas We are credibly Informed, That in many of Our Plantations, Colonies and Factories beyond the Seas, belonging to Our Kingdom of England, the Provision for Ministers is very mean, and many others of Our said Plantations, Colonies and Factories are wholly Destitute and Unprovided of a Maintenance for Ministers, and the Publick Worship of God, and for lack of Support and Maintenance for such, many of Our Loving Subjects do want the Administration of God's Word and Sacraments, and seem to be Abandoned to Atheism and Infidelity; And also for want of Learned and Orthodox Ministers to Instruct Our said Loving Subjects in the Principles of true Religion, divers Romish Priests and Jesuits are the more Encouraged to pervert and draw over Our said Loving Subjects to Popish Superstition and Idolatry.

II. And whereas We think it Our Duty, as much as in Us lies, to promote the Glory of God, by the Instruction of Our People in the Christian Religion; and that it will be highly Conducive for Accomplishing those Ends, that a sufficient Maintenance be provided for an Orthodox Clergy to live amongst them, and that such other Provision be made as may be Necessary for the Propagation of the Gospel in those Parts. *That a Maintenance for an Orthodox Clergy, and other Provision may be made for the Propagation of the Gospel in the Plantations beyond the Sea.*

III. And whereas We have been well assured, That if We would be graciously pleased to Erect and Settle a Corporation for the Receiving, Managing and Disposing of the Charity of Our Loving Subjects, divers Persons would be Induced to Extend their Charity to the Uses and Purposes aforesaid.

IV. Know ye therefore, That We have, for the Considerations aforesaid, and for the better and more Orderly carrying on the said Charitable Purposes, of Our special Grace, certain Knowledge, and mere Motion, Willed, Ordained, Constituted and Appointed, and by these Presents, for Us, Our Heirs and Successors, Do Will, Ordain, Constitute, Declare and Grant, That the most Reverend Fathers in God, Thomas Lord Archbishop of Canterbury, and John Lord Archbishop of York, the Right Reverend Fathers in God, Henry Lord Bishop of London, William Lord Bishop of Worcester, Our Lord Almoner, Simon Lord Bishop of Ely, Thomas Lord Bishop of Rochester, Dean of Westminster, and the Lords Archbishops of Canterbury and York, the Bishops of London and Ely, the Lord Almoner and Dean of Westminster, for the time being, Edward Lord Bishop of Glocester, John Lord Bishop of Chichester, Nicholas Lord Bishop of Chester, Richard Lord Bishop of Bath and Wells, Humphrey Lord Bishop of Bangor, John Montague Doctor of Divinity, Clerk of Our Closet, William Sherlock Doctor of Divinity, Dean of St. Pauls, William Stanley Doctor of Divinity, Arch-Deacon of London, and the Clerk of the Closet, of Us, Our Heirs and Successors, the Dean of St. Pauls, and Arch-Deacon of London, for the time being; The two Regius and two Margaret Professors of Divinity of both Our Universities, for the time being, Thomas Earl of Thanet, Thomas Lord Viscount Weymouth, Francis Lord Guilford, William Lord Digby, Sir Tho. *His Majesty Incorporates the Archbishop of Canterbury, and 93 others, by the Name of, The Society for the Propagation of the Gospel in Foreign Parts.*

A Cookes

Cut off from the Anglican hierarchy in England, the Anglican Church in Virginia was forced to develop its own, unique, system of church government. Vestries, comprised of influential lay members, were organized to oversee each parish. These governing bodies became a powerful force and eventually won the authority to appoint ministers as well as to set salaries. This kind of vestry, so important in Virginia, was unknown in England. The power exercised by these wealthy laymen inadvertently made ministerial positions in the colonies even less attractive to English clergymen, who preferred to stay in England where the Church was powerful enough to protect their position against encroachments mounted by the local gentry.

Anglicans in England acknowledged the problems facing the Church of England in the colonies. In 1701 the Society for the Propagation of the Gospel in Foreign Parts (SPG) was founded through the efforts of the Anglican clergyman Thomas Bray. The Society's charter stated that atheism, heathenism, and papism were spreading in the colonies for lack of ministers (figure I.2.). Money was raised and used to support Anglicanism in the New World, both where it was already established and where it was not. Because the Anglican Church had royal support, SPG missionaries were free to work anywhere in the colonies. Even where a different church was already established, as in the colony of Massachusetts, SPG ministers had to be accepted.

5
The Society for the Propagation of the Gospel in Foreign Parts.
[*Charter*].
(London, 1702)

This broadside was printed in London in 1702 to publicize the newly established Society for the Propagation of the Gospel in Foreign Parts. The Society was organized by the Church of England to collect money to finance missionary and educational efforts in the colonies. Hoping to spread Anglicanism into new areas, the organizers were also concerned to correct the deficiencies of the Church in areas where it was already established (figure I.2.).

6
Society for the Propagation of the Gospel in Foreign Parts.
An Account of the Propagation of the Gospel in Foreign Parts.
(London, 1704)

This broadside reported on the efforts of the Society during its first three years.

Each colony that benefited from the organization's ministrations was listed, along with the nature of the aid received.

7
Church of England.
Collection of Articles, Canons, Injunctions, etc.
(London, 1699)

As part of its missionary effort, the SPG sent books and other material aid to Anglican churches in the colonies. This *Collection* reprinted various documents on the beliefs and organization of the Church of England. This particular copy was sent to Trinity Church in Newport, Rhode Island, which was founded in 1702. The front cover bears a gold stamp that reads "belonging to the Church of Rhode Island." Largely through the efforts of the Society, the Newport church had a library of over one hundred volumes shortly after its founding.

I.3. Trinity Church in Newport, Rhode Island (courtesy of the Rhode Island Historical Society). The church was built in 1702. This view shows the church in ca. 1865.

Partly through the efforts of the Society, the Anglican Church was eventually introduced into every colony. Outside of the southern colonies where it was the official religion, Anglicanism appealed greatly to wealthy people living in northern cities who had increasing contact with their counterparts in England through their business and social connections. Trinity Church in Newport, Rhode Island, and King's Chapel in Boston offer two examples of Anglican churches with this sort of membership (figure I.3.). Still, despite the efforts of SPG missionaries, the Church of England was nowhere very successful, not even in its first colony, Virginia.

While in its homeland the Church of England embraced religious uniformity as the ideal and enjoyed considerable support, in America the Church of England inadvertently contributed to religious diversity. The mother country's official faith was never established on a strong enough foundation to exercise control in the colonies comparable to that in England, and Anglicanism eventually became just one faith among many. Despite the special status the Church of England enjoyed in its mother country, SPG missionaries in America had to vie for souls with the supporters of other faiths. Thus, the one church that would seem to have had the best hopes of becoming the preeminent religious institution in British North America had failed to do so. Well before the English defeat in the American Revolution dealt a crushing blow to the Church of England in America, the Church had lost any chance it may have had of commanding conformity in colonial religion. Religious homogeneity in early America was clearly off to a bad start in Virginia. Adherents of other faiths, meanwhile, were determined to try *their* hand at establishing religious conformity in a particular colony. Some even made a better beginning of it than the Anglicans had. As we know, however, their attempts were similarly doomed to failure.

8
George Keith (1639?–1716).
A Journal of Travels from New-Hampshire to Caratuck, On the Continent of North-America.
(London, 1706)

George Keith toured the American colonies as an SPG missionary in 1702–1704. He kept this journal of his travels, recounting his efforts on behalf of the Church of England. Keith, a former Quaker, focused much of his missionary zeal on that sect. At the same time, leading Quaker preachers traveled through the colonies trying to undermine his efforts. Keith's personal history gives some indication of the growing religious diversity in the colonies and, to a lesser extent, in England during these years. Born a Scots Presbyterian, Keith converted to Quakerism in the 1660s and settled in Pennsylvania in 1689. There he broke with leading Friends, and established a splinter group known as the Christian, or Keithian, Quakers. Returning to England, Keith was ordained an Anglican minister in 1700 and ended his days as the rector of a church in Sussex.

Congregational New England

The second major colonization effort mounted by the English was orchestrated as two separate ventures in the area that is now Massachusetts. The groups that settled in New England had been part of a large religious reform movement in England, a movement predicated on the idea that the Church of England had not departed enough from Roman Catholic practices. These reformers, known as Puritans, wanted to return to the practices of the early Christian church, practices they believed the Roman Catholic and Anglican churches had wrongly abandoned. They criticized the ritual used in the Anglican church services and advocated a simplified, plainer style of worship. They also considered the hierarchical organization of the Anglican Church contrary to Biblical truth and questioned the Church on its inclusiveness. Many reformers thought that only those individuals who were destined for salvation—known as the "elect" or "saints"—ought to be admitted as full members of a Church. The remainder of the populace was expected to attend church services without participating in the Protestant sacraments of the Lord's Supper and baptism. The Anglican Church, on the other hand, administered the sacraments to everyone in an effort to create a national, all-inclusive church.

English and New English Puritans differed among themselves in the definition of their relationship to the as-yet-imperfect Anglican Church. A handful of the Puritans adopted a separatist position, arguing that the Church of England was so tainted by its imperfections that it should be avoided until completely "purified." They advocated "a reformation without tarrying for any." Separatists congregated together to worship illegally in England, or else they were forced to the European continent where a Protestantism closer to their own was being practiced. After spending a dozen years in Holland, one separatist group decided to migrate to the New World instead. Led by William Bradford, who left a history of their experiences, this group of Separatists, later known as the Pilgrims, settled at Plimouth Plantation in 1620 (figure I.4.).

9
John Robinson (ca. 1575–1625).
A Just and Necessarie Apologie of Certain Christians ... Called Brownists or Barrowists.
(London, 1625)

John Robinson served as the minister to the group of English Separatists who left England to live first in the Netherlands and then in Plimouth Plantation. He died in Holland before he and the remainder of his little flock could join the Pilgrims at Plimouth. In 1619, before Plimouth was founded, Robinson published this defense of the group's beliefs and practices. This copy is a later English translation of the work, which was originally published in Latin. Robert Browne and Henry Barrow were radical Separatists of an earlier generation whose names had become epithets for all those who adopted a similar position. Thus the congregation led by Robinson was derisively labeled "Brownists" or "Barrowists."

10
William Bradford (1590–1657).
History of the Plimoth Plantation
(London, 1896)

William Bradford was one of the leaders of the Plimouth Plantation and often served as governor of the little colony. He wrote this history based on his observations over the years. A few colonists had access to the manuscript as a reference when writing histories of their own. It was later lost and then rediscovered in England early in the nineteenth century.

Most Puritans, however, chose to work within the Church of England for as long as that seemed feasible. Beginning in 1590, many brilliant and famous Puritan divines were able to preach and to publish their views. Cambridge University became a center of the reform movement. Puritans were able to retain their positions as ministers in the Church of England and to advocate reforms from the pulpits of the very churches they hoped to change. All of this came to an abrupt halt in 1633, however, when Charles I appointed William Laud to the post of Archbishop of Canterbury. Under Laud's direction, Puritan ministers were forced to conform or lose their positions, and all criticism of the Church of England was suppressed. This turn of events made it clear to many Puritans that any further efforts at reform from within were in vain.

Of Plimoth Plantation

And first of y occasion, and Indusments ther vnto; the which that y may truly vnfould, y must begine at y very roote & rise of y same. The which y shall endeuor to manefest in a plaine stile; with singuler regard vnto y simple trueth in all things, at least as near as my slender Judgmente can attaine the same.

1. Chapter

It is well knowne vnto y godly, and judicious, how euer since y first breaking out of y lighte of y gospell, in our Honourable nation of England (which was y first of nations, whom y Lord adorned ther with, after y grose darknes of popery which had couered, & ouerspred y christian worled) what warrs, & oppositions euer since satan hath raised, maintained, and continued against the saincts, from time, to time, in one sorte, or other. Some times by bloody death & cruell torments, other whiles ymprisonments, banishments, & other hard vsages: as being loath his kingdom should goe downe, the trueth preuaile; and y churches of God reuerte to their anciente puritie; and recouer, their primatiue order, libertie, & bewtie. But when he could not preuaile by these means, against the maine trueths of y gospell, but that they began to take rooting in many places; being watered with y blooud of y martires, and blesed from heauen with a gracious encrease. He then begane to take him to his anciente strategemes, vsed of old against the first christians. That when by y bloody, & barbarous persecutions of y Heathen Emperours, he could not stoppe, & subuerte the course of y gospell; but that it speedily ouerspred, with a wounderfull celeritie, the then best known parts of y world. He then begane to sow errours, heresies, and wounderfull dissentions amongst y professours them selues (working vpon their pride, & ambition, with other corrupte pasions, yncidente to all mortall men; yea to y saints them selues in some measure) By which wofull effects followed; as not only bitter contentions, & hartburnings, schismes, with other horrible confusions. But satan tooke occasion & aduantage therby to foyst in a number of vile ceremoneys, with many vnprofitable Cannons, & decrees which haue since been as snares, to many poore, & peacable souls, even to this day. So as in y anciente times, the persecuti-

I.5. *The Whole Booke of Psalmes* (Cambridge, 1640). Only eleven copies have survived of this work, the first book printed in the British colonies of North America. It was often referred to as the "Bay Psalm Book." This copy, completely intact including the binding, belonged to one of the translators of the volume, the famous Richard Mather.

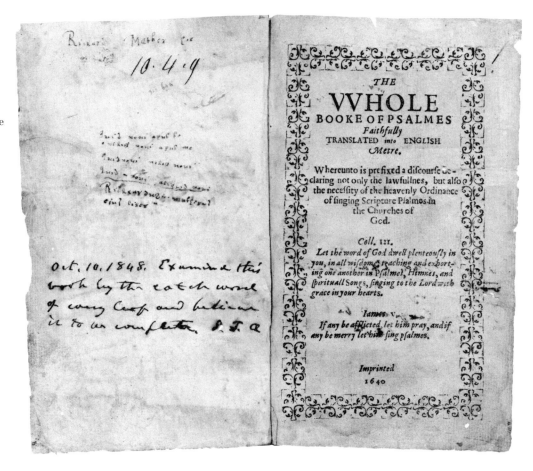

I.6. Richard Mather. Woodcut by John Foster, 1670 (courtesy of Houghton Library, Harvard University). This was the first print produced in British North America.

One of the immediate consequences of the ill-conceived policies of Charles I was the Great Migration of Puritans to New England. The majority of those who came to New England were not Separatists in the sense that the Pilgrims at Plimouth were. The Puritans in Massachusetts initially hoped to return to a reformed England someday. However, by the very act of emigrating they separated themselves from active participation in the Church of England, gathering instead Congregational churches that functioned independently. Eventually, they ceased altogether to think in terms of reforming the Church of England.

The Pilgrims settled in the southeastern area of present-day Massachusetts in 1620. Less than a decade later, non-Separatist Puritans founded a much larger and ultimately more successful colony to the north, the Massachusetts Bay Colony. The colonists in the two settlements were in agreement on most questions of religious belief and practice, and their few points of disagreement were overcome by the end of the century, when Plimouth Plantation was absorbed into its larger neighbor. In addition, both agreed with their Anglican counterparts to the south on the necessity of religious uniformity, although the religious establishment they collectively supported was quite different from that in Virginia.

With no hope of immediately reforming the Church of England, the founders of the first New England colonies worked to establish an exemplary Biblical commonwealth of their own. Their program came to be known as the "New England Way." After so many years of frustration in England, they embraced the opportunity to organize their churches and indeed their entire colony according to their religious beliefs. Each town was to have a congregational church with the power to call its own minister. Because Puritan ministers were being harried out of England, more than enough of them were available to fill these posts in the early years. Everyone in the colony was required to attend church services morning and afternoon on Sunday and to contribute to the financial support of the minister, but only those adults who could prove their sainthood to the congregation were considered full church members. These saints could participate in the sacrament of the Lord's Supper and have their children baptized. The right to vote or to hold public office in the colony was limited to the adult male church members. The colonial magistrates, once elected, were believed to have been appointed by God and were obliged to protect the church as the need arose.

In order to assure a constant supply of ministers and because they placed a high value on religious education generally, the Puritans founded Harvard College almost immediately, in 1636 in Cambridge, Massachusetts. They quickly set up a printing press, too. The first book published in the English colonies—a translation of the Psalms known as the "Bay Psalm Book"—was produced on that press in 1640 (figures I.5. and 6.). The publications of the next century continued to be largely religious in nature.

11
The Whole Booke of Psalmes.
(Cambridge, 1640)

This new translation of the Psalms was the first book published in the English colonies. The John Carter Brown Library copy was orginally owned by the minister Richard Mather, one of the translators of the work, and bears his signature (figures I.5. and 6.).

Believing that religion was of unparalleled importance and that their particular version of Christianity was correct, the New England Puritans worked to create and to preserve uniformity. Those who disagreed with the establishment were expected to keep their opinions to themselves. Anyone who openly dissented was silenced or banished from the colony. As one colonist, Nathaniel Ward, put it: all dissenters "shall have liberty to keep away from us" (figure I.7.). Like the Anglicans in Virginia, the new England Puritans endorsed the idea of religious uniformity. They, too, expected the civil magistracy to police the realm of the spirit with the strong arm of the law. Eventually they, too, were forced to tolerate a certain amount of dissent. Beginning in the 1660s, a few colonists converted to the Quaker or Baptist faith and refused to be banished from the colony or to allow themselves to be persecuted out of existence. Not until the 1720s and 1730s, however, did the colonial legislature excuse these groups from paying taxes to support the local ministry. This limited toleration, granted only grudgingly, represented the extent of the concessions offered by the majority.

In the congregational system adopted in these first New England colonies, questions of discipline and church policy were technically left up to the individual congregation. In reality, however, the congregations often worked together. One congregation might call on a few of its neighbors for assistance on some thorny question. Frequently, the colony's ministers would come together to offer advice on a more general problem.

12
Nathaniel Ward (1578–1652).
The Simple Cobler of Aggawam in America.
(London, 1647)

Nathaniel Ward served as minister of Ipswich, the Algonquin name of which was Aggawam. He was also experienced as a lawyer, having practiced in England before becoming a minister. In 1641 he had been chosen to write the first codification of Massachusetts law. This, his only other published work, defended the colonial religious establishment to English audiences. In a justly famous passage he explained the official attitude toward dissenters (figure I.7.).

13
Thomas Hooker (1586–1647).
A Survey of the Summe of Church-Discipline.
(London, 1648)

Thomas Hooker was one of the greatest Puritan divines to migrate to New England. Although renowned as a theologian, he was even more famous for his oratorical skills. Hooker served briefly as the pastor of the congregation at Newtown (later Cambridge) and then led a group out of Massachusetts to found Hartford, Connecticut. This work, published posthumously in England, explicated the theological position of the New England Congregationalists.

14
A Platform of Church Discipline.
(Cambridge, 1649)

The *Platform of Church Discipline* was issued in 1649 by a synod of Connecticut and Massachusetts churches that had been meeting in Cambridge periodically for three years. Known as the Cambridge Platform, the document outlined the ecclesiastical policies of the New England churches on seventeen different points. The final chapter addressed the question "Of the Civil Magistrates Power in Matters Ecclesiastical" and described the vigorous role the civil leaders were expected to take in protecting and promoting the interests of the church. The synod also discussed the baptism of the third generation. Unable to resolve that thorny question satisfactorily, the church leaders left it for a later council to consider.

not vent it now, feares, the pride of his own heart will dub him duns for ever. Such a one will trouble the whole *Israel* of God with his most untimely births, though he makes the bones of his vanity stick up, to the view and griefe of all that are godly wise. The devill desires no better sport then to see light heads handle their heeles, and fetch their carreers in a time, when the Roofe of Liberty stands open.

The next perplexed Question, with pious and ponderous men, will be : What should be done for the healing of these comfortlesse exulcerations. I am the unablest adviser of a thousand, the unworthiest of ten thousand ; yet I hope I may presume to assert what follows without just offence.

First, such as have given or taken any unfriendly reports of us *New-English*, should doe well to recollect themselves. We have been reputed a Colluvies of wild Opinionists, swarmed into a remote wildernes to find elbow-roome for our phanatick Doctrines and practises : I trust our diligence past, and constant sedulity against such persons and courses, will plead better things for us. I dare take upon me, to be the Herauld of *New-England* so farre, as to proclaime to the world, in the name of our Colony, that all Familists, Antinomians, Anabaptists, and other Enthusiasts, shall have free Liberty to keep away from us, and such as will come to be gone as fast as they can, the sooner the better.

Secondly, I dare averre, that God doth no where in his word tolerate Christian States, to give Tolerations to such adversaries of his Truth, if they have power in their hands to suppresse them.

B　　　　　　　　　　　　Here

I.7. Nathanial Ward. *The Simple Cobler of Aggawam in America* (London, 1647).

One particularly difficult issue arose a few decades after the Bay Colony was first planted. It revolved around the question of the status of the grandchildren of church members. The first generation had baptized the children of members, assuming that these children would grow up and demonstrate their own sainthood to their churches. When these children reached adulthood and began to have children of their own without becoming full church members themselves, a synod had to be called to discuss the problem. In 1662, the synod agreed to baptize this third generation, even though their parents were not full members. Neither the parents nor their children were eligible for communion until they were considered saints. This decision has been labeled the Half-Way Covenant because of the partial membership status of the people in question. The result of this synod was especially controversial, and a great deal of argument was necessary before it was fully accepted. Yet the concurrence of the elect on questions of belief and practices was considered fundamental, and any effort necessary to maintain consensus seemed worthwhile.

With an adequate supply of ministers from the start and a form of religious organization more loosely structured and therefore more easily transplanted to the colonies, the New England Puritans were more successful at installing a vigorous religious establishment than were their Anglican neighbors to the south. Still, both groups, despite differences of religious belief and practices, had the same ideal of uniformity in religion. In both colonies it was assumed that religious and secular leaders would work closely together to insure peace and harmony and to maintain moral standards set by the churches. Yet the New World held surprises for those who assumed that Old World standards of conformity in matters of religious practice could be carried over the ocean intact.

15
John Higginson (1616–1708).
The Cause of God and His People in New-England.
(Cambridge, 1663)

John Higginson was a second-generation New England minister. His father, Francis, had briefly been the minister in Salem years earlier. During his early adulthood John worked in Connecticut, but in 1659 he took over the pulpit previously occupied by his father. As a newly arrived and well-respected minister, Higginson was asked to deliver the election-day sermon in 1663. Every year one man was honored by an invitation to preach on this occasion to the colony's gathered leaders. These sermons usually addressed the important issues of the day and were often published. Higginson's *The Cause of God and His People in New England* is the oldest published election day sermon of which copies have survived. Its title reflected the belief among orthodox New Englanders that God had chosen them to establish true Christianity in the New World. In the sermon Higginson delineated those things which were not included in God's cause: materialism, separation, and toleration.

16
Increase Mather (1639–1723).
A Discourse Concerning the Subject of Baptisme.
(Cambridge, 1675)

This work has been described as the most able defense of the Half-Way Covenant. Increase Mather, also a second-generation New England minister, had initially rejected the Half-Way Covenant in opposition to his own father, Richard, and many other ministers. The battle among the ministers on this theological issue was won once the younger Mather reversed his position and came out in support of this innovation. In addition to this weighty treatment of the subject, Increase also published *The First Principles of New-England Concerning Baptism & Communion of Churches* in the same year. By quoting extensively from earlier works, that essay attempted to demonstrate that the first generation would have been in agreement with the Half-Way Covenant. With Mather's reversal, agreement among the ministers had been achieved, and Increase worked to prove that there had never been any real cause for conflict. Nevertheless, many lay people were not certain of the wisdom of this change. Eventually, disagreements within the orthodox establishment opened the door to diversity, despite efforts by the Mathers and others to maintain consensus.

II.1. John H. Cady. Map of the State of Rhode Island Showing Territorial Bounds for the Years 1636–1659 (courtesy of the Rhode Island Historical Society). Rhode Island was originally composed of numerous plantations or settlements, most of which had different religious orientations. This map, drawn in 1936, shows the early settlements under the leadership of Roger Williams (Providence), Anne Hutchinson (Portsmouth), William Coddington and John Clarke (Newport), and Samuel Gorton (Warwick).

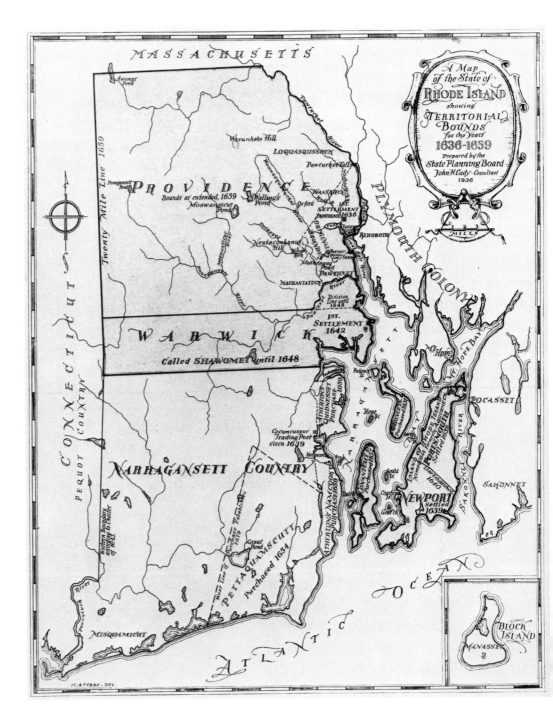

CHAPTER II

Rhode Island Introduces Diversity

While Anglicans in Virginia and Congregationalists in Massachusetts were determined to continue the English practice of maintaining a religious establishment in North America, the settlers of Rhode Island pioneered the religious diversity that would eventually characterize all the colonies. Rhode Island was settled in response to the intolerant policies of the Bay Colony Puritans. In their quest for a truly godly state the Massachusetts Bay Colony was prepared to banish any individual who voiced views that did not conform to their own understanding of God's will. Particularly during the early years, when hopes of creating a Bible commonwealth were still high, a number of people were driven out of the colony.

Roger Williams

Of these religious rebels, the first and most important was Roger Williams. Born the son of a London shopkeeper, Williams was educated at Cambridge University through the patronage of the distinguished jurist Sir Edward Coke. After he finished his schooling, he was appointed chaplain in the household of Sir William Marston. Such chaplaincy positions allowed wealthy reform-minded families to hear "plain style" Puritan preaching when the local pulpit was filled by someone with High Anglican sympathies.

When Massachusetts was being chartered, Williams decided to participate in its Puritan colonization venture. Arriving in Boston early in 1631, he refused a call to minister to the church there because the congregation had not declared itself separated from the Church of England. Instead, Williams chose to settle in Plimouth where the Separatist beliefs of the congregation were more in accord with his own views. Williams and his young family lived in Plimouth for just two years before he received a call to Salem, Massachusetts, ten miles north of Boston, where the church had adopted a Separatist position.

In Salem he continued to advocate Separatism for all Massachusetts churches and quickly became embroiled in other controversies as well. Williams argued that the King of England had no right to give away land in New England; that the oath of all but the "saints," the members of the elect, was blasphemous; and that the magistrates should not concern themselves with breaches of the first four commandments, which address the individual's relationship to God. Thus Williams challenged the very basis of the colonization venture—the land titles granted by the King—as well as that of the Puritans' scheme for creating a Bible commonwealth—the government's role in assuring religious conformity.

Although the Salem church records relating to Williams's two years there have been lost, it is clear that his unconventional views had the support of some of the townspeople. Fearing that he might collect a major following, and unable to silence him in any other way, the authorities of the Bay Colony banished him from the colony in 1635. Williams fled south during the winter of 1635–36 to avoid deportation back to England, where his extreme views would have met with severer punishments. Joined by a handful of supporters from Massachusetts, he founded the town of Providence that summer (figure II.1.).

Both as leader of a new settlement and as a deeply religious man, Williams was in a position to erect a government in accord with his own vision of a godly state. Yet, unlike his Puritan contemporaries in the other New England colonies, Williams did not embrace this opportunity. Instead, he stood by his belief that coercion ought never be used in matters of faith. Williams reasoned that because humanity was inherently sinful and imperfect, no individual could ever be certain that his own views were correct and thus have the right to force his beliefs on others. The best that could be hoped for in this imperfect world was that each person would be able to pursue his own version of the truth. Most people, Williams believed, would fail in this search, because most of humanity was destined for eternal damnation. But the saved, or the elect, need not be concerned with the misguided struggles of the unregenerate so long as these lost souls obeyed all civil laws and did not try to force their beliefs on anyone else. Williams therefore differed from his associates in the other northern colonies in being a radical in social philosophy as well as in religious views: he combined the radical Protestantism of all Puritans with the idea that social harmony could be maintained without coercion in matters of faith. Naturally, this "soul liberty," as he called it, attracted many other settlers whose unorthodox beliefs made them unwelcome elsewhere in New England. From the first, then, Rhode Island was remarkable for the religious diversity it attracted and for its lack of a single established religion.

As for Williams, he continued his quest for personal spiritual fulfillment. In 1639 he joined with other settlers in gathering a Baptist church in Providence (figure II.2.). After just six months he left that church, and from that time on remained independent of any organized religion. Williams could most accurately be described as a "seeker," the contemporary term for one who rejects all sectarian affiliations but constantly seeks a community of the faithful able to live up to the high standards of a pure religious fellowship. Williams's own experiences confirmed his belief that individuals had to be free to find their own way, a position he defended against the orthodox view in a debate with a leading Massachusetts minister, John Cotton. Williams's greatest work, *The Bloudy Tenet, of Persecution, for Causes of Conscience* (1644), in which he presented his views on the proper relationship between church and state, grew out of this debate. Williams even went so far as to suggest that liberty of conscience be granted to Roman Catholics, an idea few Protestants anywhere at that time would have entertained.

Although a lifelong advocate of soul liberty, Williams himself had strong convictions about theology. He could defend soul liberty and at the same time, and with equal energy, attack another person's doctrines as contrary to Scriptural truths: the freedom to express opposition to any specific constellation of beliefs was one of the major benefits of soul liberty. In 1672, as an old man, Williams participated in a four-day-long debate with three traveling Quakers (figure II.3.). By this time the Quakers were numerous in Rhode Island, particularly in Newport, and Williams challenged them to a debate. Accounts of the event were written by both sides, and in them we can see the vehemence with which the Calvinist Williams went after the "perfectionist" Quakers. But at no point in the proceedings did Williams advocate taking civil action against the sectaries. He preferred instead a public forum in which thoughts could be exchanged and, perhaps, minds changed.

Nearly every aspect of Roger Williams's life was shaped by these innovative

II.2. The Baptist meetinghouse in Providence, as depicted in 1789 in the *Massachusetts Magazine*, volume I, number 8. The Baptist church in Providence, usually recognized as the first in America, was organized in 1639. This meetinghouse was constructed in 1774–1775.

17

Roger Williams (ca. 1603–1683).
The Bloudy Tenet, of Persecution, for
Cause of Conscience, discussed, in a
Conference betweene Truth and Peace.
(London, 1644)

Williams's greatest work, *The Bloudy Tenet*, laid out his belief in the importance of liberty of conscience. Williams's views were presented in a dialogue between truth and peace, who eventually agreed that religious persecution was contrary to the principles of both. The work was published as part of a debate with the Boston minister John Cotton while Williams was in London securing a charter for Rhode Island. *The Bloudy Tenet* was hastily written and printed, but the work has rightly been called Williams's masterpiece. Appearing in England during its civil war, when such questions were openly discussed for the first time, this work secured Williams's reputation as an able proponent of religious radicalism.

18

John Cotton (1584–1652).
The Bloudy Tenet Washed, and Made White
in the Bloud of the Lambe: Being Dis-
cussed and Discharged of Bloud-
Guiltinesse by Just Defence.
(London, 1647)

John Cotton was possibly the most famous Puritan minister to join in the Great Migration to New England. He had preached in Boston, England, until he was ejected from his living in 1633. On his arrival in New England, he was immediately asked to serve as teacher of the Boston church, a post he held for the rest of his life. The sectaries who gathered around Anne Hutchinson a few years later in Boston praised Cotton as one of the few godly ministers in the colony, and he shared some of their views about the importance of grace in the spiritual life of a Christian. If Cotton ever toyed with the idea of adopting the radical mysticism of Hutchinson and her supporters, he was dissuaded by the combined efforts of his fellow ministers. Afterwards, he helped to defend the New England Way against all comers. This tract represented Cotton's best effort against Roger Williams's arguments for liberty of conscience, although it was by no means Cotton's best work. In it, he argued that heretics sinned against their own consciences in adopting their erroneous views.

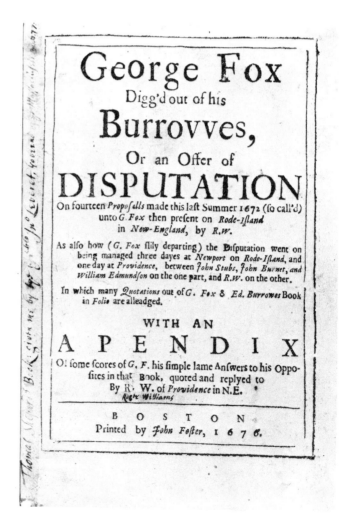

II.3. Roger Williams. *George Fox Digg'd Out of His Burrowes* (Boston, 1676). The inscription along the left side of the page reads: "Thomas Shepard's Book: given me by the hon[or]able Jno Leveret, Governor of the Massachusetts 30.6.77." Shepard (1635–1677) was the teacher at the Charlestown church when the Governor gave him this book.

19

Roger Williams (1604?-1683).
George Fox Digg'd Out of His Burrowes.
(Boston, 1676)

In 1672, when the Quaker leader George
Fox was touring the American colonies,
Roger Williams challenged him to a debate.
The letter containing the challenge and
the fourteen points Williams suggested for
debate arrived too late to catch Fox, but
three other traveling witnesses agreed to
meet with Williams in his stead. The dispu-
tation took place in Newport and Providence over four days before large
audiences. After it was over, Williams
published this account of the confrontation. Nowhere was his ability to advocate
both liberty of conscience and an unyield-
ing set of his own personal beliefs more
strikingly demonstrated than in this

pamphlet, the only work by Williams
published in America during his lifetime.
Its title puns on the names of two early
Quaker leaders, George Fox and Edward
Burroughes. The orthodox Congregationalists who controlled the press in Boston
may have disagreed with Williams on many
issues, but they approved of his attack on
Quakerism. As Calvinists who believed
that man was naturally depraved and that
only a few were saved, they found objectionable the Quaker idea that anyone could
be guided by the "Christ within." That
Williams's treatment of the subject was
considered acceptable in the colony from
which he had been banished some forty
years earlier is demonstrated by the inscription in the John Carter Brown
Library copy.

20

George Fox (1624-1691) and John Burnyeat
(1631-1690).
A New-England Fire-brand Quenched.
([London], 1678)

The Quakers replied to Williams's
pamphlet in kind, coming out with this
work two years later. John Burnyeat had
been one of three debaters on the Quaker
side, while Fox was the man Williams had
originally challenged. The vehemence of
the language on both sides was typical of
the pamphlet exchanges on religious subjects during this era.

21

Roger Williams.
A Key into the Language of America.
(London, 1643)

The *Key,* published in 1643, was one of the
fruits of over a decade of extensive contact
that Willams had had with southern New
England Indians. Ostensibly a dictionary
of Algonquin words and phrases and their
English meanings, the book was full of
anecdotal accounts or "observations."
English audiences were intrigued by the
thought of Williams, a well-educated
Englishman, living among the "savages."
Unlike most of the other Europeans who
came to America, Williams was able to
respect and appreciate Native American
culture.

ideas. His unprecedented attitudes toward Native American beliefs are a case
in point. While both the Anglicans and Puritans, with rare exceptions, tended
to dismiss Indian religion as nonexistent or as mere pagan superstition, Williams
was interested in studying and understanding Indian beliefs. He often traveled
among the Algonquins trading, negotiating, or visiting and thereby learned a
great deal about their culture. His most popular work, *A Key into the Language
of America* (1643), was the result of his exposure to various southern New
England tribes (figure II.4.). The work revealed Williams's bias in favor of Protestant Christianity, certainly, but it also demonstrated his belief that the individual can find truth with only a minimum of institutional assistance. He was
pleased to observe that his Indian neighbors, though they lacked even the
Scriptures as a guide, held many beliefs that were similar to his own. This
startling discovery increased his respect for the culture of these indigenous
Americans and his conviction that the human spirit is better left unfettered.
Williams was, perhaps, the only educated colonist willing and able to cross the
cultural barrier between English and Native Americans in early New England.
The reasons he was able to do so were intimately related to the convictions
that made him an advocate of liberty of conscience for all and a seeker in his
own spiritual life.

Of their Religion. (124–125)

Maunaûog Mishaûnawock.	*Many, great many.*
Netop machàge.	*Friend, not so.*
Paûsuck naûnt manìt.	*There is onely one God.*
Cuppíssittone.	*You are mistaken.*
Cowauwaûnemun.	*You are out of the way.*

A phrase which much pleaseth them, being proper for their wandring in the woods, and similitudes greatly please them.

Kukkakótemous, wáchit-quáshouwe.	*I will tell you, presently.*
Kuttaunchemókous.	*I will tell you newes.*
Paûsuck naûnt manìt kéesittin keesuck, &c	*One onely God made the Heavens, &c.*
Napannetashèmittan naugecautúmmonab nshque.	*Five thousand yeers ago and upwards.*
Naûgom naûnt wukkesittínnes wáme teâgun.	*He alone made all things.*
Wuche mateàg.	*Out of nothing.*
Quttatashuchuckqúnnacaus-keesitínnes wáme.	*In six dayes he made things.*
Nquittaqúnne. Wuckéesitin wequâi.	*The first day Hee made the Light.*
Néesqunne. Wuckéesitin Keésuck.	*The second day Hee made the Firmament.*
Shúc...	
Shúckqunne wuckéesitin Aûke kà wechêkom.	*The third day hee made the Earth and Sea.*
Yóqunne wuckkéesitin Nippaûus kà Nanepaûshat.	*The fourth day he made the Sun and the Moon.*
Neenash-mamockíuwash wêquanantíganash.	*Two great Lights.*
Kà wáme anócksuck.	*And all the Starres.*
Napannetashúckqunne Wuckéesittin pussucksecíuck wáme.	*The fifth day hee made all the Fowle.*
Keesuckquíuke.	*In the Ayre, or Heavens.*
Kà wáme namaûsuck.	*And all the Fish in the Sea.*
Wechekommíuke.	
Quttatashúkqunne wuckkéesittin penashímwock wamè.	*The sixth day hee made all the Beasts of the Field.*
Wuttàke wuchè wuckeesittin paûsuck Enìn, or, Eneskéetomp.	*Last of all he made one Man*
Wuche mishquòck.	*Of red Earth,*
Kà wesuonekgonnakaûnes Adam, túppautea mishquòck.	*And call'd him Adam, or red Earth.*

K 3   Wuttàke

22
Thomas Morton (1575–1647).
New English Canaan.
(Amsterdam, 1637)

Thomas Morton was one of a handful of Englishmen already living in New England when the *Mayflower* arrived at Plimouth Plantation. Nominally an Anglican and most certainly anti-Puritan, Morton was soon driven from the region. One of his offenses had been selling arms to and keeping company with the local Indian tribe. He wrote *New English Canaan* to avenge himself against the colonists. His work has primarily been of interest for his detailed descriptions of the land and its original inhabitants. Although Morton was befriended by some of the local Indians, his assessment of their religion was typically eurocentric; according to Morton, in fact, native Americans had no religion.

23
Ralph Hamor, the younger.
A True Discourse of the Present Estate of Virginia.
(London, 1615)

Anglican settlers in Virginia displayed little more appreciation of Native American religion than did their counterparts in the northern colonies. No marriage between a European and an American attracted greater attention than that between the English settler John Rolfe and the Indian "princess" Pocahontas. In this early description of colonial Virginia, Ralph Hamor reprinted a letter from John Rolfe to his superior about the marriage. High on Rolfe's list of motives for desiring to marry Pocahontas was his ambition to convert her from her heathen state, not to mention the strategic benefits such an alliance would bring to the infant colony. Despite the many good reasons Rolfe could find to marry, he experienced a great deal of mental anguish before deciding that God had called upon him to save her soul. If Rolfe could perceive anything of value in the culture of his new wife, he kept that information to himself.

24

John Eliot (1604–1690), translator.
*Mamusse Wunneetupanatamwe
Up-Biblum God.*
(Cambridge, 1663)

John Eliot, the Puritan missionary to the Indians, translated the Bible into an Algonquin dialect as part of his labors (figure II.5.). The task, which involved developing a written language as well as translating the entire Bible into that language, took more than a decade to complete. A printer and press had to be sent from England to publish the work because the press at Harvard College was inadequate to a task of this magnitude. This was the first Bible printed in the English colonies in any tongue, and its publication marked the high point of the limited Puritan efforts to convert Massachusetts Indians to Christianity. Unfortunately, the dialect Eliot used was not even comprehensible to all the local tribes, and the overall impact of his Bible on Native American belief was minimal. Eliot's attitude toward the people he worked so hard to convert was implicit in the program he instituted, which was described by his friend and colleague Thomas Shepard.

25

Thomas Shepard (1605–1649).
The Clear Sun-Shine of the Gospel Breaking forth Upon the Indians in New-England.
(London, 1648)

Eliot's Indian Bible was one element in his program to convert the Indians living in Massachusetts to Christianity. So called "Praying Indian" villages, where the converted would live under English supervision, constituted a second aspect of the program. The villages were never very successful in attracting converts and lasted only until English animosity toward Native Americans of any faith flared up during King Philip's War in 1675. In the 1640s, when the villages were just being established, a number of tracts describing missionary efforts were published to inform English backers and others of the progress of the project. *The Clear Sun-Shine* served as a sequel to John Wilson's *The Day Breaking if not the Sun-Rising of the Gospel with the Indians in New England*, published the year before. Both ministers took care to reprint the rules governing the Christian Indian villages. These regulations revealed the emphasis placed on inculcating English cultural norms as if these were but one aspect of Christianity. Most of the English perceived Native American culture and religion as something worthless and even threatening, to be discarded as soon as possible.

II.5. The Bible translated into an Algonquian language by the Massachusetts minister John Eliot. This was the first Bible printed in America in any language. The New Testament was published in 1661 and the Old Testament in 1663, both in Cambridge, Massachusetts.

The Hutchinsonians

During the years after Williams founded Providence, a number of other dissenters from the New England Way settled in the area that would eventually become the colony of Rhode Island. Soon after banishing Williams, Massachusetts was confronted with another threat to the religious uniformity of the colony. The source of this threat was a newly arrived matron named Anne Marbury Hutchinson. When the Reverend John Cotton was silenced in England and decided to emigrate to Massachusetts, many members of his congregation followed him across the ocean in order to remain under his pastoral care. Hutchinson, who arrived in Boston in 1634 with her husband and their numerous dependents, was among these followers.

Hutchinson, who was later described by one of her detractors as "a woman of ready wit and bold spirit," soon became an important part of the social and religious life of Boston. As the mistress of a substantial household who also perhaps served the community as a midwife, she had a certain amount of influence at the outset which she parlayed into a spiritual following of her own. She began holding religious meetings in her home, where she would discuss the sermons preached by the town's ministers. She became increasingly critical of some, and claimed that a regenerate person, a member of the elect, could distinguish the saved from the damned in this life. The evidence of salvation, she argued, was not good behavior or good "works." Salvation was effected by grace, and those who were in a truly gracious state were recognizable to each other as such. Hutchinson's emphasis on grace over, or even to the exclusion of, works won her the label of "antinomian," that is, one who considers himself above the moral law embodied in the Old Testament. Although Hutchinson could rightly be labeled a "spiritist" by her contemporaries because of the emphasis she placed on the workings of the spirit, the epithet "antinomian" exaggerated her position in order to discredit her.

Many Bostonians supported Hutchinson, including the colony's new governor, Sir Henry Vane, and her brother-in-law, the Reverend John Wheelwright. Because of the size of her following and the high status of some of her supporters, a bit of political maneuvering was necessary before Hutchinson and her staunchest advocates could be banished from the colony. In 1637, Hutchinson was examined before both a civil court and the Boston church, and was banished and excommunicated in turn. Many of her followers were disarmed, disenfranchised, and in some cases, also banished.

A sizable group of these Hutchinsonians removed south to settle with Williams's assistance in Portsmouth in 1638, not far from Providence (figure II.1.). There they were free to worship as they pleased. Hutchinson and a few others preached to the settlers, but apparently no church was formally gathered for a time. Having advocated a more mystical version of Christianity than that being practiced in the Bay Colony, the Hutchinsonians were generally receptive to the opportunities for spiritual experimentation their new circumstances afforded. Although the group did not endorse diversity in principle and even tried to implement their own version of a Bible commonwealth, those hopes foundered quickly. Soon they were searching for truth in many directions, ultimately settling upon a number of different religious creeds. Hutchinson's followers remained Congregationalists or adopted new faiths, most notably Quakerism and, to a lesser extent, Baptist Protestantism. The careers of John Clarke and William Coddington—two of the men who had supported her against the Massachusetts establishment—are illustrative.

Clarke and Coddington were among the leaders of a group that splintered off from the Portsmouth settlement soon after arrival and went on to establish

John Winthrop (1588–1649).
*A Short Story of the Rise, Reign and Ruin
of the Antinomians, Familists & Libertines.*
(London, 1644)

John Winthrop, a wealthy squire by birth
and lawyer by profession, left England in
1630 as one of the leaders of the Great
Migration. Once in Boston, he frequently
served as governor or deputy governor of
the infant colony. He kept a journal that is
one of the richest sources for the early
history of Massachusetts. Winthrop led the
opposition to Anne Hutchinson. This tract,
published anonymously in England in 1644,
presented the orthodox side of the battle
with Hutchinson. Thomas Weld, who edited
the work, wrote the preface, and arranged
for its publication, interpreted Hutchinson's recent death at the hands of Indians
on Long Island as a divine judgment
against her and her views. Winthrop was
no theologian, and his account lacked some
of the subtlety that the colonial ministry
brought to the debate. But it revealed the
personal animosities, political maneuvering, and sense of crisis that accompanied
the controversy.

John Wheelwright, Jr. (1592?–1679).
*Mercurius Americanus, Mr. Welds his
Antitype.*
(London, 1645)

John Wheelwright was one of the Puritan
ministers silenced by the bishops in
England. Shortly after his arrival in New
England in 1636, he found himself at the
center of the antinomian controversy. The
brother-in-law of Anne Hutchinson, he was
nominated by the Hutchinsonians to the
post of teacher in Boston's church.
Winthrop successfully opposed the ap-
pointment, and Wheelwright left Boston to
minister to the people living at Mount Wol-
laston. He remained in close contact with
his friends in Boston, however. The following year, the General Court announced a
day of fasting and repentence to resolve
the disagreements that divided the town.
Wheelwright attended the afternoon lec-
ture by John Cotton, after which he delivered an unscheduled, provocative sermon
of his own. His subsequent conviction for
sedition was the first in a series of civil
actions against the Hutchinson group which
ended in Anne's banishment. The publication of Winthrop's *A Short Story*, which
cast him in an unflattering light, seemed
unfair to Wheelwright, given that he had
already publicly apologized. In the title of
this pamphlet, Wheelwright expressed his
ire at Thomas Weld for arranging the London printing of the work.

the town of Newport (figure II.1.). Clark, a physician with some university training, had arrived in Boston after the controversy over Hutchinson's views had
reached its peak. He immediately identified with Hutchinson and joined the
migration to Narragansett Bay. Once in Newport, he became a Particular (or
Calvinist) Baptist and the minister of a congregation there. In 1651 he suffered
punishment in Boston with two other Rhode Island Baptists for returning to
that colony to minister to a Lynn resident who requested his services (figure
II.6.). Later he paid a brief visit to England and joined the Fifth Monarchy Men,
a militantly radical religious sect. In the 1660s he petitioned the King on behalf
of Rhode Island to permit the colony to "hold forth a lively experiment, that a
fluorishing civill state may stand, yea, and best be maintained...with a full
liberty in religious concernments." This request was granted in 1663, when
Rhode Island's new charter instituted freedom of conscience. Clarke, who was

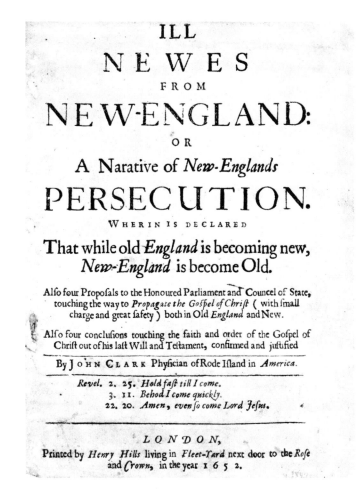

ILL
NEWES
FROM
NEW-ENGLAND:
OR
A Narative of *New-Englands*
PERSECUTION.
WHERIN IS DECLARED
That while old *England* is becoming new, *New-England* is become Old.

Alſo four Propoſals to the Honoured Parliament and Councel of State, touching the way to *Propagate the Goſpel of Chriſt* (with ſmall charge and great ſafety) both in Old *England* and New.

Alſo four concluſions touching the faith and order of the Goſpel of Chriſt out of his laſt Will and Teſtament, confirmed and juſtified

By J o н n C l a r k Phyſician of Rode Iſland in *America*.

Revel. 2. 25. *Hold faſt till I come.*
3. 11. *Behod I come quickly.*
22. 20. *Amen, even ſo come Lord Jeſus.*

LONDON,
Printed by *Henry Hills* living in *Fleet-Yard* next door to the *Roſe* and *Crown*, in the year 1 6 5 2.

a close associate of Roger Williams, continued as pastor of the Newport church until his death in 1676. In John Clarke, the Hutchinsonians had someone who ultimately rivaled Williams himself as an apostle of soul liberty.

William Coddington, a wealthy merchant, had served as a magistrate in the Bay Colony before siding with Hutchinson. In that capacity he had a hand in banishing Williams, just a few years before he himself was ostracized. In Rhode Island his leadership abilities were recognized, and he was elevated to the Old Testament office of judge over the settlers on Aquidneck Island. He led the faction that founded Newport and later served for many terms as governor over the colony. Although Roger Williams had arranged the gift of Aquidneck for the newly arrived settlers, Coddington considered Williams his rival. For a time he even tried to maintain the island as a separate settlement. But Coddington enjoyed the opportunities inherent in the soul liberty Williams promoted, exercising it two decades later when he became a Quaker. A powerful member of the large Newport Quaker community that included many of Hutchinson's followers, Coddington used his influence throughout New England in support of Quakerism. He enjoyed chastising his old friends and associates in Massachusetts for their treatment of him and other dissenters. As two of Hutchinson's most renowned followers, Clarke and Coddington were apparently fairly typical of that group in their willingness to leave the Congregationalism of the New England Puritans altogether in order to embrace another sect. The settlers on Aquidneck contributed to the religious diversity of Rhode Island over the years by taking their quest for spiritual truths in whatever direction it happened to lead them.

John Clarke (1609–1676).
Ill Newes from New-England.
(London, 1652)

Trained as a minister and as a physician, Clarke arrived in Boston in the middle of the uproar surrounding Hutchinson's dramatically successful lay ministry. He participated in the initial settlement at Portsmouth, Rhode Island, in 1638 and was one of the founders of Newport the following year. Like many other radical Protestants, Clarke came to question the practice of infant baptism and began to embrace Anabaptist views. He ministered to the Baptist church at Newport from its founding until his death. In 1651 he traveled to Lynn, Massachusetts, in the company of two other Newport Baptists,

John Crandall and Obadiah Holmes. William Witter, an aged, blind Lynn resident with Baptist sympathies, had requested the ministrations of the Newport church. The three men were apprehended by authorities in Massachusetts, tried, and ordered whipped or fined. Holmes, a former Salem resident who had already been convicted for preaching in Plimouth Colony, spent some time in jail. Clarke published this tract to call attention to the intolerance of the Bay Colony and to defend the right to liberty of conscience against Massachusett's policies (figure II.6.). Clarke would later play a major role in winning Rhode Island the assurance of this liberty in the royal charter of 1663.

William Coddington (1601–1678).
A Demonstration of True Love.
([London], 1674)

Another of Anne Hutchinson's followers, William Coddington, assumed various leadership positions, first in Massachusetts and then in Rhode Island. He was possibly the wealthiest man in Boston during the confrontation, and later became one of the most powerful men in Rhode Island. Like many other Hutchinsonians, Coddington became a Quaker during the 1650s. He subsequently used his influence with other New England leaders (particularly the tolerant Connecticut resident, John Winthrop, Jr.) to disseminate Quaker tracts and to advocate the Quaker cause. This,

his only published work, was written in response to the uncooperative reaction his efforts received from his old friend, Richard Bellingham. Coddington had sent a letter to Bellingham, then governor of Massachusetts, through a Quaker who had recently taken up residence in Boston. Bellingham refused to read the letter, burning it unopened, and briefly placed Nicholas Moulder in custody for delivering it. *A Demonstration of True Love* related that incident, printed the text of the original letter, and recounted the long history of intolerance in New England. Coddington reminded Bellingham of their former friendship, and urged repentance, toleration, and Quakerism on the governor.

Samuel Gorton

A third group to take shelter in the more tolerant colony of Rhode Island, after being poorly received elsewhere in New England, consisted of Samuel Gorton and his followers. Gorton left London, where he worked as a clothier, to come to Massachusetts early in 1637. Arriving in the midst of the antinomian controversy, Gorton moved immediately to Plimouth Plantation where he soon found himself in trouble for lay preaching, criticizing the government, and advocating various "heretical" beliefs. He was banished from Plimouth and went to join the Hutchinsonians at Aquidneck. For a time Gorton's mystical bent made him attractive to many of the settlers in Portsmouth, but provocative attacks on Coddington and the other magistrates resulted in his expulsion from that area as well. Next, the irrepressible Gorton went to Providence, where he became involved in land disputes. Finally, he and the supporters he had attracted along the way settled further south in Shawomet (now Warwick) (figure II.1.).

In Shawomet Gorton mistakenly believed he had finally found a place to live unmolested. In fact, his difficulties with the Massachusetts authorities were just beginning. Acting on the complaint of two Indian sachems, the authorities brought Gorton and a number of others to trial in Boston for heresy and attacking

II.7. Sir Henry Vane the younger (1613–1662) (courtesy of the Rhode Island Historical Society). Vane lived in Massachusetts briefly and was elected governor during the conflict over Anne Hutchinson's ministry. After the Hutchinson faction was defeated, he returned to England where he eventually became involved in the radical religious and political movements developing there. A friend of Roger Williams's and of many other New World radicals, Vane was executed after the Restoration as a regicide.

the government. The Gortonists were narrowly spared the death penalty, but were sentenced to hard labor in leg irons in various Massachusetts towns. This punishment backfired when a few colonists became "infected" with Gortonist beliefs, with the result that the offenders were released and allowed to return to Shawomet. Gorton later returned to England for a short time and there published an attack on the Bay Colony.

Gorton was far more radical in his religious views than even Williams or Hutchinson. While Williams questioned civil intervention in matters of faith, Gorton challenged all forms of government as man-made and therefore insufficient. Hutchinson agreed with Gorton on the importance of grace as opposed to works, but she did not—as did Gorton—think that Christ was literally present in the saints. Although his ideas made Gorton an uncooperative participant in any civil state, he was able to live out his life in Shawomet/Warwick. Williams included his settlement, along with those on Aquidneck, in the patent he requested for the colony in 1644. "Gortonism" did not become a lasting sect, but the Gortonists were able to remain in the colony and contributed to the religious diversity there.

In less than a decade of growth the area around Narragansett Bay had half a dozen English settlements (figure II.1.). The settlements were colonized haphazardly by three different groups and so had no legal status beyond that bestowed by land deeds signed by leaders of the Narragansett tribe. Aware that the neighboring colonies of Plimouth, Connecticut, and Massachusetts were scheming to encroach on the area in an effort to rid New England of this collection of religious rebels and to acquire the land for themselves, Roger Williams went to England to arrange a charter for the settlements.

The situation in the mother country had changed substantially since the Great Migration had begun more than a decade earlier. Civil war had disrupted civil and religious institutions, leaving Parliament in the hands of radicals, and the Church of England in complete disarray (see chapter III). In 1644 Williams was able, with the help of his friend Sir Henry Vane, to obtain a patent uniting the various settlements in the area as the "Providence Plantations" (figure II.7.). With the colony legally organized, the settlers enjoyed a degree of protec-

30
Samuel Gorton (1592–1677).
Simplicities Defence Against Seven-Headed Policy.
(London, 1646)

Samuel Gorton was one of the most unconventional figures in early New England. At one time or another he came into conflict over questions of religion and land ownership with every colony in southeastern New England. During the 1640s he pub-

lished numerous doctrinal tracts that revealed his radical stance on almost every topic. His views were similar to those held by many English radicals during the same period, and he won the support of some temporarily powerful individuals in his battles with various colonial authorities. In this tract, Gorton presented his case against the New Englanders he had tangled with during the preceding decade.

31
Nathaniel Morton (1613–1685).
New Englands Memoriall.
(Cambridge, 1669)

As a nephew of Plimouth leader William Bradford, Morton had access to Bradford's manuscript history "Of Plimoth Plantation" while preparing this account of the early years of New England. *New Englands*

Memoriall was the first history published in the colonies, and it described all the various and sundry dissenters who had rebelled against efforts to achieve religious uniformity. Morton presented, among other subjects, the orthodox version of Gorton's conflict with the authorities of Plimouth and Massachusetts.

tion from their unfriendly neighbors. In addition, the colony's inhabitants were empowered to determine their own religious policies, a choice they exercised in 1647. The residents of Providence Plantations agreed that "all men may walk as their consciences persuade them, everyone in the name of his God." Within two decades John Clarke was instrumental in arranging a second charter that superseded the first. The 1663 royal charter for the colony of "Rhode Island and Providence Plantations" granted liberty of conscience. With this unprecedented royal sanction for its "lively experiment," Rhode Island was well launched on its career as the maverick among the English colonies.

Shocked critics of the colony dubbed it "Rogue's Island," "that cesspool of New England," and other insulting epithets, but the colony continued on its unconventional way. Even though it was proving impossible to achieve complete religious uniformity anywhere in the colonies, the attachment to the ideal died hard. That Rhode Island had actually embraced the principle of liberty of conscience from the first was difficult for conservative advocates of the necessity of civil supervision over spirtual affairs to accept, much less approve. At the end of the century, the learned Boston minister and Puritan polemicist Cotton Mather contemptuously attacked Rhode Island for this policy (figure II.8.). Mather's penchant for rhetorical flourishes aside, his contempt and outrage was shared by many others who viewed the colony as being irreligious and proud of it. Still, the example set by Rhode Island would prove to be a harbinger of the future. To the dismay of the advocates of religious conformity throughout the colonies, diversity and, finally, religious freedom were to become the norm (figure II.9.).

32
The Charter Granted by His Majesty King Charles The Second to the Colony of Rhode Island and Providence Plantations.
(Boston, 1719)

The charter granted to Roger Williams by Parliament in 1644 was nullified with the Restoration of the Stuart monarchy in 1661. The colony had to petition the King for a new charter, and this request was granted in 1663. Charles II chose to permit the policy of freedom of conscience to continue in force in Rhode Island. This was the first royal charter specifically to grant this freedom.

33
Cotton Mather (1663–1728).
Magnalia Christi Americana.
(London, 1702)

A Boston minister and the son and grandson of three leading colonial clergymen, Cotton Mather epitomized the Puritan ministry of his age. He had something to say on every subject, and published more than any other man in the English colonies. His magnum opus was a history of New England called *Magnalia Christi Americana.* Packed with information and Mather's opinions on many topics, the *Magnalia* related the tale of the trials and triumphs of the Puritans in New England— without, however, mentioning Rhode Island. Only in book seven, which was reserved for all the savages, witches, heretics, and criminals who had tried to undermine the saints' experiment, did he finally treat Rhode Island in detail. If the positioning of the material on Rhode Island did not make Mather's point strongly enough, he had a few unkind words to say about the colony as well. Striving to maintain consensus and uniformity against the increasing dissent and diversity of his age, Mather was particularly critical of the colony that had always maintained the liberty of conscience he so deeply distrusted (figure II.8.).

Lesser; of several Figures; few of any *Perfect*, none of any *Humane* Shape. This was a thing generally then Asserted and Believed; whereas, by some that were Eye-witnesses, it is affirmed, that these were no more *Monstrous Births*, than what it is frequent for Women, labouring with *false Conceptions*, to produce. Moreover, one very nearly Related unto this Gentlewoman, and infected with her Heresies, was on *October* 17, 1637. delivered of as hideous a *Monster* as perhaps the Sun ever lookt upon. It had no *Head*; the *Face* was below upon the Breast; the *Ears* were like an *Apes*, and grew upon the Shoulders; the *Eyes* and *Mouth* stood far out; the *Nose* was hooking upwards; the *Breast* and *Back* were full of short Prickles, like a *Thorn-back*; the *Navel*, *Belly*, and the Distinction of Sex, which was Female, were in the place of the *Hips*; and those *Back-parts* were on the same side with the *Face*; the *Arms*, *Hands*, *Thighs* and *Legs*, were as other Childrens; but instead of *Toes*, it had on each Foot three *Claws*, with Talons like a *Fowl*; upon the *Back* above the *Belly* it had a Couple of great *Holes* like Mouths; and in each of them stood out a Couple of pieces of Flesh; it had no *Forehead*, but above the Eyes it had *Four Horns*; Two of above an Inch Long, Hard and Sharp; and the other Two somewhat Less. The Midwife was one strongly suspected of *Witchcraft*; and a prime *Familist*: Thro' whose *Witchcrafts* probably it came to pass, that most of the Women present at the Travel were suddenly taken with such a violent Vomiting and Purging, tho' they had neither Eaten or Drunken any thing to Occasion it, that they were forced immediately to go Home; others had their Children so taken with *Convulsions*, which they never had before or after, that *they* also were sent for Home immediately; whence none were left at the time of the *Monster's* Birth, but the *Midwife* and *Two* more, whereof one was fallen asleep: And about the time of the *Monster's* Death, which was Two Hours before its Birth, such an odd *Shake* was by invisible Hands given to the Bed as terrify'd the Standers-by. It was Buried without any Noise of its *Monstrosity*; but it being whispered a few Days after about the Town, the Magistrates ordered the opening of the Grave, whereby there was discovered this

Monstrum, Horrendum, in forme, Ingens.

But of this *Monster*, good Reader, let us talk no further: For at this Instant I find an odd Passage in a Letter of the famous Mr. *Thomas Hooker* about this Matter; namely this, *While I was thus Musing, and thus Writing, my Study where I was Writing, and the Chamber where my Wife was sitting, shook, as we thought, with an Earthquake, by the space of half a quarter of an Hour. We both perceived it, and presently went down. My Maid in the Kitchen observed the same. My Wife said, it was the Devil that was displeased that we confer about this Occasion.*

§. 12. It was but a few Years after these things, namely in the Year 1643. that the Government of *Barbados* being disturbed by such Turbulent and Tumultuous *Familists*, as those which now pestered *New-England*, were forced by their Outrages to sentence them with *Banishment*. Nor must it be made a Reproach, if *New-England* also ordered a sort of *Banishment* for these intoxicated Sectaries, who began to Deny or Degrade the *Magistracy* of the Country, and call the King of *England*, the King of *Babylon*; but you shall hear the effect of that Procedure. Being advised of an *Island* beyond *Cape-Cod*, and near the *Narraganset-Bay*, they fairly purchased it of the Natives; thither they transplanted themselves with their Families; in this Transplantation, accompanied by many others of their own *Uncertainty* in Religion; who yet had not come under any *Censures* of either the Court or the Church for their Misdemeanours. Having peopled this Island, now known by the Name of *Rhode Island*, they swarmed over unto the Main, where they also purchased some Tracts of Land, now covered with the Two Towns of *Providence* and *Warwick*; for all of which they obtained at last a *Charter* from King *Charles* II. with ample Priviledges. I cannot learn that the First Planters of this Colony were agreed in any one Principle so much as this, *That they were to give one another no disturbance in the Exercise of Religion*; and tho' they have sometimes had some Difference among them, as to the Exercise of that Principle also, I believe there never was held such a variety of *Religions* together on so small a Spot of Ground as have been in that Colony. It has been a *Colluvies* of *Antinomians*, *Familists*, *Anabaptists*, *Antisabbatarians*, *Arminians*, *Socinians*, *Quakers*, *Ranters*, every thing in the World but *Roman Catholicks*, and *Real Christians*, tho' of the *Latter*, I hope, there have been more than of the *Former* among them; *so that if a Man had lost his Religion, he might find it at this general Muster of Opinionists!* 'Tis a good Peice of *Antiquity* that *Josephus* has given us, when he tells us the Consequences of *Nehemiah's* chasing away a Son of *Jojada*, the Son of *Eliash* the High-Priest, for Marrying the Daughter of *Sanballat* the *Horonite*, the chief Person among the *Samaritans*. The Father-in-law of this *Menasses* (for it seems that was his Name) built a Temple on *Gerizzim*, in Opposition to that at *Jerusalem*, and obtained a Charter from the Kings of *Persia* for the Encouragement thereof, that so his Daughter *Nicaso* (for so she was called) might not lose her Husband, who was thus made a *Metropolitan*. After this time, all that were Indited for Crimes at *Jerusalem* would fly to *Gerizzim*, and *Sichem* was now the common Receptacle and Sanctuary of Jewish Offendors: This, as R. *Abrah. Zaccuth* tells us, *This was the beginning of Heresie!* And now, with some Allusion to that Piece of Antiquity, I may venture to say, That *Rhode Island* has usually been the *Gerizzim*

II.9. *The Rhode Island Almanack for the Year 1728* (Newport, 1727). In keeping with the acceptance of religious diversity in Rhode Island, this almanac listed the annual meetings for both Baptists and Quakers throughout the northern colonies. The product of the press of James Franklin, who set up shop in Newport after being harried out of the less tolerant colony of Massachusetts, this almanac was one of the first works printed in Rhode Island. James Franklin's far more famous younger half-brother, Benjamin, learned the printer's trade from James in Boston before running away to Philadelphia, where he demonstrated a similar willingness to work with diverse religious groups. This illustration is from a facsimile of the 1727 imprint published in 1911.

Of the ECLIPSES, 1728.

THIS Year affords four Eclipses, two of the Sun, and Two of the Moon.

The First is an Eclipse of the Moon, on our 14th *February*, about Two in the Morning, the Moon being then in the South-West; a little better than one Third of her Body will be darkned.

The Second is of the Sun, *February* 28, and will last from about Three to Five Afternoon. About Five Digits will be darkned, and will be worthy your strict Observation, if Clouds do not interpose.

As for the other two, they are both invisible (to wit, one of the Moon, on the 8th of *August*, and one of the Sun on the 23d of *August*,) they both happening out of our Hemisphere.

The Sun, the Moon, the Stars, do all fulfil
Unto a Tittle their Creator's Will.
The glorious Sun's created for our Light,
And constantly performs his Office right;
Until th' eternal Night o'th' World come on,
When th' World and we are all together gone.

Quakers General-Meetings are kept.

March 17.	At *Philadelphia*.	Aug. 25	At *Westbury*.
April 28.	At *Salem*.	Sept. 15.	At *Philadelphia*
May 26.	At *Flushing*.	22.	At *Jamaica*.
June 16.	At *Providence*.	Oct 13.	At *Choptank*.
10.	At *Newport*	27.	At *Shrewsbury*.
23.	At *Newtown*.	27.	At *Oyster-Bay*.
9.	At *West-River*	Nov. 24.	At *Flushing*.
July 28.	At *West-Chester*.	Feb. 25.	At *Westbury*.

Baptist's General Meetings are kept.

May 12.	At *Welsh-Tract* in *Newcastle* County.		
19.	At *Cohanfie*.	Sept 22.	At *Philadelphia*.
June 2.	At *Piscataqua* in *New-Jersey*.		

CHAPTER III

English Civil-War Sects in America

While Anglicans and Congregationalists were trying to create viable religious establishments in the New World, the situation in England took a brief, but startling, turn away from religious uniformity. The vigorous policies of King Charles I's appointee, Archbishop Laud, resulted in the exile of some people to New England, and the harassment of many more. In addition, Charles adopted a number of unpopular economic and political policies. Parliament refused to cooperate in voting money for the crown, so the King tried unsuccessfully to rule without parliamentary support. Parliament seized the initiative in 1640, and soon the country was divided into royalists (supporters of the King) and parliamentarians. After a civil war resulted in victory for the latter, the King and the archbishop were executed as traitors early in 1649. Leadership of the nation eventually fell to a Puritan general in the parliamentary army, Oliver Cromwell, who adopted a policy of almost complete religious freedom, with the government favoring no particular faith. He ruled until his death in 1658, when his son Richard made a feeble effort at succeeding him. The monarchy was finally restored, with some of its old authority curtailed, in 1660.

For the two exciting decades of this period of upheaval, the people of England experienced an unprecedented degree of religious freedom. Radical ideas that had earlier been suppressed came out in full force, while new ideas and movements also emerged. A plethora of new sects – Ranters, Seekers, Quakers, Levelers, Diggers – joined with Baptists, Congregationalists, and Presbyterians in openly expressing their views. The diversity in Rhode Island anticipated on a small scale the explosion of religious groups that rocked England during the 1640s and 1650s.

It was this change that made it possible for such New World radicals as Roger Williams, John Clarke, and Samuel Gorton to publish their works in England. The orthodox New England colonies, once looked upon as a bit too radical by members of the English establishment, were now chastised for their conservative intolerance. Even their closest allies within the English religious spectrum, the Independents (or Congregationalists), advised the Bay Colony leaders to show more restraint in dealing with dissenters. They saw that Cromwell's religious policy had increased their own freedom, even if it also benefited other, more extreme, sects. As startling as this temporary transformation in England was to many observers in the New World, the lasting impact of these years is to be found in the fact that several of these civil-war sects ultimately took root in America.

Ephraim Pagitt (1575?–1647).
Heresiography.
(London, 1661)

During the English civil war many sects flourished in England. With the religious establishment dissolved, the monarch executed, and the censorship laws revoked, radical religious ideas were freely discussed and adopted. Supporters of orthodoxy were appalled by the events of these decades. Ephraim Pagitt's *Heresiography,* which described all the various sects in highly disapproving terms, went through six printings from 1645 to 1661. His treatment of those he considered heretics reflected the hostile reaction of many to the religious freedom enjoyed during this era. In order to buttress arguments against religious liberty, orthodox observers like Pagitt related scandalous rumors of the murders and orgies in which Ranters, Quakers, Baptists, and others reputedly participated (figure III.1).

III.1. Ephraim Pagitt. *Heresiography: or a Description of the Heretickes and Sectaries Sprang Up in these Latter Times.* 6th edition. (London, 1661).

III.2. Edward Johnson. *A History of New-England. From the English Planting in the Yeere 1628 untill the Yeere 1652* (London, 1654). This work is more commonly known by its running title, "Wonder-working Providence."

ly and humble walking, have you not the most blessedest oper-tunity put into your hands that ever people had? then

---

CHAP. V.
What Civill Government the People of Christ ought to set up, and submit unto in New England.

FAyle not in prosecution of the Worke, for your *Lord Christ* hath furnished you with able Pilots, to steere the Helme in a godly peaceable, Civill Government also, then see you make choyce of such as are found both in Profession and Confession, men fearing God and hating bribes ; whose Commission is not onely limitted with the commands of the second Table, but they are to looke to the Rules of the first also, and let them be sure to put on *Joshuas* resolution, and courage, never to make League with any of these seven Sectaries.

First, the *Gortonists*, who deny the Humanity of Christ, and most blasphemously and proudly professe themselves to be per-sonally Christ.

Secondly, the *Papist*, who with (almost) equall blasphemy and pride prefer their own Merits and Workes of Supererogation as equall with Christs unvaluable Death, and Sufferings.

Thirdly, the *Familist*, who depend upon rare Revelations, and forsake the sure revealed Word of Christ.

Fourthly, *Seekers*, who deny the Churches and Ordinances of Christ.

Fifthly, *Antinomians*, who deny the Morrall Law to be the Rule of Christ.

Sixty, *Anabaptists*, who deny Civill Government to be proved of Christ.

Seventhly, The *Prelacy*, who will have their own Injunctions submitted unto in the Churches of Christ. These and the like your Civill Censors shall reach unto that the people of, and un-der your Government, may live a quiet and peaceable life in all godlinesse and honesty, and to the end that you may provoke Kings, Princes, and all that are in authority to cast downe their Crownes at the Feet of Christ, and take them up againe at his command

35
Edward Johnson (1598–1672).
A History of New-England.
(London, 1654)

Edward Johnson's *History of New-England* recorded the disapproving reaction of the Massachusetts establishment to the events in England. Johnson, a joiner by trade, came to New England during the 1630s and helped to found the town of Woburn in 1640. He served in various public offices and was a leading layman in the colony. In 1650 he began writing this history which described the special care God took of His chosen people in Massachusetts (figure III.2.). Johnson, distressed by develop-ments in England, denounced all views aired there that were not in accord with his own Congregationalism. In an ironic turn of events, two of Johnson's own chil-dren later converted to sects their father had so strenuously attacked.

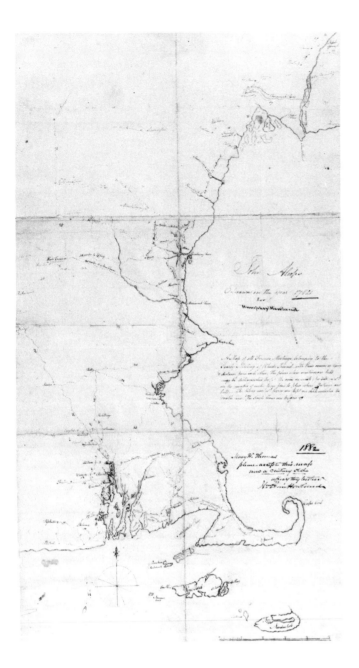

III.3. Drawn in 1782, this manuscript map pinpoints the location of all Friends Meetings belonging to the Yearly Meeting of Rhode Island.

Quakers

In both England and America the most successful of the new sects, in terms of longevity and impact, was the group known as the Quakers. The Quakers, who later adopted the name Society of Friends, believed that each individual possesses an Inner Light that provides sure guidance in spiritual matters. This light was thought to embody the same spirit as that contained in Scripture, and many believers hoped that the very fact of its shining again, after so long, heralded the end of the world.

Itinerant preachers, most notably George Fox, began spreading the word about the Inner Light throughout England in the late 1640s, and the sect quickly won many converts. In the mid-1650s Quaker witnesses began traveling outside of England, going as far as the Middle East and the British colonies. Wherever the traveling witnesses went, colonists were converted, with the first large New World Quaker community springing up in Rhode Island.

Outside Rhode Island, the Quakers met with varying degrees of persecution. Their critics feared that their disregard for established religion, educated ministers, some of the finer points of theology, and certain standards of civil government (such as the swearing of oaths in judicial proceedings) would lead to irreligion and even anarchy. Massachusetts was the most severe in its persecution, executing four Quakers in the years between 1659 and 1661. One of these martyrs to the Quaker cause was the Rhode Island matron Mary Dyer, who had left Massachusetts in 1638 as one of Anne Hutchinson's leading supporters.

After the Restoration of the Stuarts to the throne of England in 1660, the King pressured the colonists into putting an end to the most severe forms of persecution. Still, the Quaker sect was harassed for many years to come in England and much of the New World. In the late 1660s George Fox introduced more organization and structure into the movement, developing a system of meetings and clearly defined disciplinary procedures. In 1672 he made a major tour of the colonies, visiting Quaker communities from Virginia to Rhode Island.

Later in the 1670s English Quakers launched a substantial migration to West Jersey, which had come under the control of a group of wealthy and influential Quaker converts. This colonization effort, although successful on a small scale, was dwarfed by the colony of Pennsylvania, established in 1681. The land was granted to William Penn to repay debts Charles II owed to his father. Penn accepted the colony with hopes of making a "Holy Experiment" on the banks of the Delaware. Although liberty of conscience was instituted in Pennsylvania at the outset, the colony was initially dominated numerically and in many other ways by the Society of Friends. Philadelphia became the leading colonial city for a time, and Quakers throughout the colonies eventually took a prominent role in the anti-slavery movement. The Society of Friends, established during the turbulent years of the English civil war, was the only sect born in the period to survive and flourish (figure III.3.).

36
George Fox.
A Journal or Historical Account.
(London, 1694)

George Fox was the son of a weaver and was trained as a shoemaker. At the age of twenty-four he began preaching publicly to anyone in England who would listen. Fox and a number of others preached that everyone should listen to the truth within for spiritual guidance. In 1652 Fox convinced a group of Seekers at Swarthmore Hall in Lancaster, including the mistress of the household, Margaret Fell. Fox and Fell later married and together provided a stable center for the growing Quaker movement. After the Restoration, Fox emerged as the preeminent leader of this radical sect. For the remainder of his life he worked to erect a sound structure for the Society of Friends. Fox and his associates organized a series of yearly, quarterly, and monthly meetings, a system for certifying traveling witnesses, and a network connecting Quakers all over the world. Fox traveled extensively himself, encouraging the adoption of these policies and procedures, and generally offering his guidance and support to the convinced. His *Journal* described his life and labors for the cause of truth. First published in 1694 and republished many times, the *Journal* served as both a history of the early movement and an inspirational tract for Friends.

37
George Bishop (d. 1668).
New-England Judged, by the Spirit of the Lord.
(London, 1703)

George Bishop had been a captain in Cromwell's army and an early convert to Quakerism. During the 1650s and 1660s he collected accounts from traveling Quakers as they came through the port of Bristol where he lived. Using information gathered from various people who had been in New England, he wrote this account of the persecution of the Quakers in the colony. The most dramatic incidents Bishop recorded were the executions of four Quakers, three men and one woman, in Boston in 1659–1661. *New-England Judged* was first published in two parts in 1661 and 1667, then abridged and reprinted for a later generation of readers in 1703.

William Penn (1644–1708).
A Perswasive to Moderation to Church Dissenters.
([London, 1686])

Penn was the son of a great admiral and a member of the English gentry. As a young man he converted to Quakerism and was among the first male members of his social class to join the sect. During the 1670s he promoted the settlement of West Jersey by English Quakers. In 1681 he convinced Charles II to grant him a tract of land in America to clear a £16,000 debt the King owed to the Penn family. Pennsylvania was thus established as a Quaker venture. William Penn played a significant part in organizing the colony's government, land distribution, and policy of religious equality. He published a number of works during his life, most notably a devotional piece, *No Cross, No Crown*. In *A Persuasive to Moderation*, he advocated the liberty of conscience he so actively promoted in both West Jersey and Pennsylvania.

Robert Barclay (1648–1690).
An Apology for the True Christian Divinity.
(Newport, 1729)

Robert Barclay, a Scottish convert to Quakerism, is considered the Society's greatest seventeenth-century theologian. His *Apology* defended the Quaker faith against its detractors and provided inspiration to many generations of the convinced. The *Apology* was immensely popular and was reprinted many times and published in six languages, of which the John Carter Brown Library owns all but the Arabic edition. This particular edition was financed by the Rhode Island Yearly Meeting of the Society of Friends and was among the first books ever published in Rhode Island. This copy was owned by the substantial Quaker merchant and philanthropist Abraham Readwood (later Redwood), who noted on the inside cover the page numbers for the topics that most interested him. Among other things, Readwood wanted a ready reference to the passages in which Barclay explained the origins of the name "Quaker" and the reasons religious ecstasy at times caused people to quake (figure III.4.).

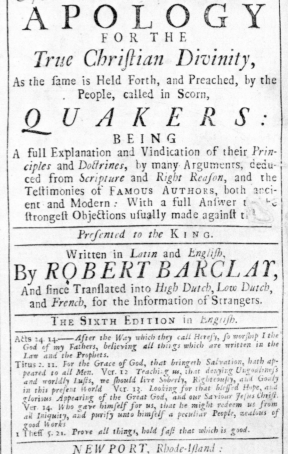

III.4. Robert Barclay's *Apology* for the "People, called in Scorn, Quakers," was first published in Amsterdam in Latin in 1676 and quickly became the standard defense of the Friends' theology. The copy illustrated here, from the sixth edition published in Newport in 1729, belonged to the Rhode Island merchant and philanthropist Abraham Redwood.

Ranters

The radical sect known as the Ranters, which also appeared during the English civil war, was far less successful than the Quakers. Because the Ranters never developed into a lasting distinct group, their ideas and practices are somewhat difficult to uncover. During the brief period in which they flourished in England, Ranters claimed (with Samuel Gorton) that God was literally in every godly person. They further reasoned that it was impossible for even the most heinous act committed by such a saintly individual to be a sin. According to their detractors, these beliefs led them to all sorts of wild behavior; hence they were given the name Ranters.

While no direct connection has been found between this English sect and a group of religious extremists who were active on Long Island during the 1670s, the Long Island group was described as Ranters by all the observers who left any record of them. Originally led by Thomas Case, "Case's Crew" became infamous for their seemingly irreligious practice of singing, dancing, and making sport of religious subjects. The group was never interested in discussing their beliefs, however, and left no written accounts of their views.

Many of the surviving accounts of the sect came from the pens of traveling Quaker witnesses, since for years the Long Island Ranters disrupted Quaker meetings in the area, singing and shouting until the proceedings were brought to a halt. Ranters, like the Gortonists they resembled in some respects, did not make a lasting impression on the American colonies. For a time, however, they did contribute to the range of possibilities for religious belief and practice found there.

40
Increase Mather (1639–1723).
An Essay for the Recording of Illustrious Providences.
(London, 1684)

It was common during the seventeenth century for people to believe that God took an active part in their daily lives. Roger Williams named his settlement on Narragansett Bay for the divine assistance, or providence, that carried him safely to his destination. The Puritan historian Edward Johnson used God's *Wonder-Working Providence* (figure III.2.) as the organizing conception of his history of Massachusetts. Thirty years later, the Boston minister Increase Mather set out to collect stories about God's activities in New England. Fearing a decline in religiosity, Mather hoped to buttress his cause by demonstrating that God did intervene directly in human affairs. The *Essay*, which was largely anecdotal, was Mather's most popular work, published twice in Boston and once in London in a single year. One of the stories recounted was that of the "Singing and Dancing Quakers" of Long Island. Mather told of the wild antics of this group of Ranters, and then went on to describe the various ways God had punished them for their irreligion. That Mather classified this marginal group as part of the Quaker movement was an embarrassment to the Society of Friends. The Quaker activist George Keith shortly challenged Mather on this score, disclaiming any connection between the two.

41
William Edmundson (1627–1712).
Journal.
(London, 1715)

Traveling Quaker preachers often kept journals of their experiences. These were frequently published posthumously to commemorate their lives and to inspire and inform others. Such journals developed into a distinct genre of Quaker devotional literature and were exceedingly popular. William Edmundson was one such traveling Friend who left an account of his work in the colonies and in Ireland. Like many other traveling witnesses, he encountered the Long Island Ranters who pestered the Quaker meeting there. Whether the Ranters shared the conservative's idea that they were part of the Quaker movement is unclear. They may have singled out the local Quakers for harassment for reasons other than a simple desire to draw them in the direction of the radical stance of Ranterism. In any case, the Society was adamant that this group was not part of their organization, and traveling Friends made that point clear in their journals (figure III.5.).

quainted her, and she had divulged the same to her Father; for which, he said, they had taken away his Wife. I ask'd, *How he could join with them in opposing me; and at such a time when I was but One, being a Stranger, and they Abundance in Opposition?* Also, *Whether it was not unmanly to do so?* But it being late, I desir'd some further Discourse with him in the Morning, which he assented to; but although I was up before the Sun rose, he was gone away before.

I sent to the Officer, that had the Charge of me the Day before, to know, if he had any further to do with me, who said, I might go when and where I pleas'd. So I paid the People for my Nights Lodging, and being clear of the Service there, I went towards the Place where I left *James Fletcher* and our Horses; in the mean time *James Fletcher* came another way to look for me: thus we miss'd of one another. When he came to *Hertford*, he heard by several where I was gone, and so came back, and told me, *That I had set all the Town a Talking of Religion.*

[margin: W. E. discharged from his Confinement.]

The next Morning we took our Journey towards *Long-Island*, and in three Days came there, where Friends received us gladly; but were much troubled in their Meetings with several who were gone from Truth, and turn'd *Ranters*, i. e. *Men and Women who would come into Friends Meetings, Singing and Dancing in a rude manner*, which was a great Exercise to Friends. We staid in that Part amongst Friends for some time, and had large and precious Meetings at several Places; many of those *Ranters* came to Meetings,

[margin: Long-Island.]

[margin: Ranters disturb Friends Meetings.]

ings, yet the Lord's Power was over them in his Testimony, and chain'd them down: some of them were reach'd with it, and brought back to the Truth, to own Condemnation for their running out into Liberty and Wickedness.

When we were clear of that Quarter, we took Boat to *East-Jersey*, and came to *Shrewsbury*, where we staid some Meetings, and were refresh'd with Friends in the Lord; from thence went to *Middletown*, and had a Meeting there, at *Richard Hartshorn's*, which was full and large; to which there came several of those People, that were tainted with the *Ranting Spirit*. One *Edward Tarff* came into the Meeting with his Face black'd, and said, *It was his Justification and Sanctification*; also sung and danc'd, and came to me, where I was sitting waiting on the Lord, and call'd me *Old rotten Priest*, saying, *I had lost the Power of God*; but the Lord's Power fill'd my Heart, and his *Word* was powerful and sharp in my Heart and Tongue, I told him, *He was mad, and that made him fret*; he said, *I lyed, for he was moved of the Lord, to come in that manner to reprove me.* I look'd on him in the Authority of the Lord's Power, and told him, *I challeng'd him, and his God that sent him, to look me in the Face one Hour, or half an Hour*; but he was smitten, and could not look me in the Face, so 'went out. The Lord's Power and Sense of it was over the Meeting, in which I stood up, and appealed to the rest, *Whether this was not the same Power of God, in which I came amongst them at the first, unto which they were directed and turned, when they were convinc'd of the Truth,*

[margin: East Jersey. Shrewsbury.]

[margin: Middletown.]

[margin: Richard Hartshorn.]

[margin: Edw. Tarff a Ranter opposes W.E.]

[margin: W. E. challenges Edward Tarff a Ranter to look him in the Face.]

III.5. William Edmundson. *A Journal of the Life, Travels, Sufferings, and Labour of Love in the Work of the Ministry* (London, 1715), with comments on the Ranters.

Rogerenes

A third sect to appear in the English colonies in the latter half of the seventeenth century was the Rogerenes. Although not technically an English sect, the Rogerenes were influenced by sectarian ideas emanating from England at mid-century. John Rogers (1648–1721), a son of a wealthy New London, Connecticut, man, joined the Westerly, Rhode Island, Seventh Day Baptist church in the mid-1670s. Soon Rogers began entertaining more radical beliefs, which the Baptists described as "Quaker-like." Faced with these disagreements over beliefs, plus the Baptists' hesitancy about continuing the rebaptism of converts to their faith (a practice opposed by the Connecticut authorities), Rogers broke with the church to establish his own sect in 1677.

Rogerenes held an eclectic assortment of Baptist, Quaker, and other views, which Rogers proclaimed to the world in strident, apocalyptic language (figure III.7.). Despite frequent court appearances and occasional prison confinements, the Rogerenes remained active in the New London area for more than a century. They carried on the tradition of radical sectarian activity long after the Quakers had accommodated to the conventions of civil society and the Ranters had ceased to exist. Although they drew upon English radical religions, the Rogerenes were perhaps the first indigenous American sect.

42
John Rogers (1648–1721).
An Epistle Sent from God to the World, Containing the best News that ever the World Heard. And Transcribed by John Rogers a servant of Jesus Christ.
([New London?], 1718)

Although John Rogers and later his son and namesake both took leadership roles in the sect, the Rogerenes apparently did not believe in having an established ministry – even women were permitted to speak in their meetings. John Rogers was harassed and persecuted for his role in the sect, spending some time in prison. He published numerous pamphlets that urged the reader to repent, heralded the coming millennium, and chastised the authorities for the ill-treatment the Rogerenes received. As the title of this tract suggested, Rogers believed that he received God's word directly, and simply transcribed it and had it printed for more general consumption (figure III.6.).

43
Samuel Bownas (1676–1753).
An Account of the Life, Travels, and Christian Experiences in the Work of the Ministry of Samuel Bownas.
(London, 1761)

Samuel Bownas, another traveling Quaker who left a journal, recounted a conversation he had with John Rogers while they were detained in a Hempstead, Long Island, jail. Bownas found that the group, which was sometimes labeled the Rogerene Quakers, did in fact share a number of beliefs with the Society of Friends. Here he related the beliefs Rogers professed, contrasting them with his own.

An
EPISTLE
Sent from GOD
to the World, Containing
the beſt News
that ever the World heard.

And tranſcribed by *John Rogers* a Servant of *Jeſus Chriſt.*

1. *Joh.* 1. Chap. and 4th Verſe.
And theſe things write we unto you, that your joy may be full.

An Introduction in order to an Expoſition upon the 1. *Chap.* of the firſt Epiſtle of *John.*

BUt before we enter upon the Expoſition of it, let us premiſe theſe following particulars: In the firſt place let

A

III.6. Published in New London, Connecticut, in 1718 by the founder of the Rogerenes, this tract presented a text that Rogers claimed he received directly from God.

The English civil war and the interregnum period that followed created turmoil in society and religion. Many extremely radical ideas were openly debated, and a few new religious sects, most notably the Quakers, were permanently established. These ideas and sects contributed to a marked expansion in the range of religious thought and activity in both England and the colonies. It was during this era, too, that the English monarchy's hopes of achieving complete religious uniformity were shattered. The Church of England was reinstituted as the official faith in 1660 and the most extreme sects forced to disband or to go underground, but the government never again attempted a repression of dissenters such as that sponsored by the late King Charles I. With the Toleration Act of 1689, many dissenting groups were free to worship, although there were still limits placed on their participation in the civil state. During the English civil war and interregnum, and again after 1689, England moved beyond some of its colonies in the toleration of dissent. Eventually, however, British North America would surpass England both in the range of religious beliefs and practices that it encompassed and in the freedom its citizens enjoyed.

IV.1. The wood engraving on the title page of John Graunt's *Truths Victory Against Heresie* (London, 1645) provided an illustrated key to the varieties of heresy, as seen from the point of view of an English Puritan.

CHAPTER IV

Beyond English Protestantism

Various forms of English Protestantism dominated the British American colonies: there were Anglicans, Congregationalists, Baptists, Gortonists, Quakers, Ranters, Rogerenes, and even a few independent Seekers like Roger Williams. Yet people of non-Protestant faiths and non-English background were also coming to the North American colonies. With their strikingly different faiths or ethnic origins, the significance of these groups for the development of religion in America far exceeded their actual numbers.

Roman Catholics

When one considers the history of the Western hemisphere as a whole, Roman Catholicism was by far the single most portentous religion brought to the New World. The initial discovery and exploration of the Americas was largely the work of European Catholics. Spain and Portugal for a time aspired to divide the rest of the world between them along the lines demarcated in a papal decree. England's major rivals in the drive to control the Americas were all Roman Catholics. The former colonial possessions of Spain and France still retain much of their religious heritage.

Yet Catholicism did not become a major religious denomination in English-speaking North America until well into the nineteenth century. Not only were the English colonists generally Protestant, they were also quite often intensely anti-Catholic. The transition from Catholicism to Anglicanism in England had not been smooth. Protestants lost their lives during the brief reign (1553–1558) of Queen Mary, known among Protestants as "Bloody Mary" for the gruesome measures she resorted to in her unsuccessful effort to return the nation to Catholicism. The tales of the martyrs and exiles for the Protestant cause were retold innumerable times, encouraging anti-Catholic sentiment. The wars of Europe were fought along religious lines during this era, and the spectacle of Protestants fighting "papists" (as Catholics were derisively called) kept these hostile attitudes alive (figure IV.1.).

44
John Graunt (fl. 1640–1652).
Truths Victory.
(London, 1645)

Anti-Catholicism was an established tradition in England by the time of the English civil war. All but a few of the country's Catholics and a handful of Anglicans agreed that Roman Catholics constituted a huge threat to England and to true religion.

In *Truths Victory* John Graunt numbered Catholics first among heretics, connecting them to various European sects (figure IV.1.). Sectarians were equally likely to associate Anglicans or moderate Puritans with Catholics in their own denunciations. In England to label someone a papist was almost universally accepted as an insult during this era.

45

The Character of A Turbulent, Pragmatic Jesuit and Factious Romish Priest.
(London, 1678)

This anonymous pamphlet offers another good example of English anti-Catholicism. It was in a series sparked by fears about the monarch's pro-French and pro-Catholic sympathies and by rumors of a popish plot to assassinate the King. The resulting tense political situation continued for a few years, and at one point a number of suspected conspirators were killed. This particular crisis subsided, but anti-Catholic feeling flared up again in the next decade. In 1687 the new king, James II, himself a Catholic, granted liberty of conscience to all his co-religionists. At the same time his wife bore him a son, assuring a Catholic heir to the throne. Protestant fears of a resurgence of Catholicism in England led the country's political and religious leaders to invite the King's Protestant son-in-law, William of Orange, to invade England. William marched virtually unopposed on London, James was allowed to escape, and Protestantism reigned in England once again. This bloodless coup was dubbed the "Glorious Revolution" by relieved English Protestants everywhere.

46

John Nalson (1638?–1686).
Foxes and Firebrands: Or, a Specimen of the Danger and Harmony of Popery and Separation.
(London, 1682)

This tract, written by an Anglican, was issued twice during the decade before the Glorious Revolution. Nalson described the papists' "restless design" to regain England, and equated Protestant dissenters with Catholics in their determination to undermine the Church of England. His title may be referring to the pamphlet debate between George Fox and Roger Williams during the previous decade. "Foxes" may have had another meaning as well, for Jesuit priests were suspected of subverting the English public with their fox-like cleverness.

47

Cotton Mather (1663–1728).
The Way of Truth Laid Out.
(Boston, 1721)

Although he was a dissenter from the Church of England, Boston minister Cotton Mather agreed with the Anglican John Nalson about the dangers posed by wily papists. His *Way of Truth Laid Out* was intended as a handy reference for Congregationalists to use in their attacks against popery. Mather then went on to explain the arguments against Anabaptists, Quakers, and other Protestant sects. Anti-Catholicism remained strong in New England throughout the colonial period. As late as 1774 the British policy of granting freedom of worship to French Catholics in newly conquered Quebec caused an uproar.

English foreign policy was often understood in terms of this religious rivalry. The Pope and the various Catholic monarchs hoped to bring England back to the fold, and for every clandestine effort they actually mounted, zealous English Protestants imagined ten more. Any concessions to Catholics by the monarchy were viewed with suspicion. When Charles I married the Catholic French princess Henrietta Maria, he moved a giant step forward toward the civil war and his own execution.

Despite this extreme hostility toward Catholics in England, some families clung to their traditional faith. During the 1630s, these people were given an opportunity to leave England and to settle in Maryland. Charles I granted that colony's charter to the second Lord Baltimore, one of the few Catholic members of the English aristocracy. In order to ensure that the colony would be safe for his fellow believers, Lord Baltimore allowed freedom of religion to any Christian who settled there.

A Jesuit priest, Father Andrew White, accompanied the first group of settlers to the colony. The first Catholic mass in an English colony was said by him when they arrived in Maryland. Although Father White wrote of this celebration

(2.)

some Cherries: That they had also some Orange and Limon trees in the ground, which yet thriued: Also, Filberds, Hazel-nuts, and Almonds; and in one place of the Colony, Quince-trees, wherewith they could furnish his Lordship; And in fine, that his Lordship should not want any thing that Colony had.

On the 3. of *March* wee came into *Chesapeake* Bay, and made sayle to the North for *Patoemeck* riuer, the Bay running betweene two sweet lands in the channell of 7. 8. and 9. fathome deepe, 10. Leagues broad, and full of fish at the time of the yeere; It is one of the delightfullest waters I euer saw, except *Potoemeck*, which wee named Saint *Gregories*. And now being in our owne Countrey, wee began to giue names to places, and called the Southerne Point, *Cape* Saint *Gregory*; and the Northerly Point, Saint *Michaels*. This riuer, of all I know, is the greatest and sweetest, much broader then the *Thames*; so pleasant, as I for my part, was neuer satisfied in beholding it. Few Marshes, or Swampes, but the greatest part sollid good earth, with great curiosity of woods, which are not choaked vp with vnder-shrubbs, but set commonly one from the other, in such distance, as a Coach and foure horses may easily trauell through them.

At the first looming of the ship vpon the riuer, wee found (as was foretold vs) all the Countrey in Armes. The King of the *Paschattowayes* had drawen together 1500. bowe-men, which wee our selues saw; the woods were fired in manner of beacons the night after; and for that our vessell was the greatest that euer those *Indians* saw, the scowtes reported wee came in a Canow, as bigge as an Iland, and had as many men as there bee trees in the woods.

Wee sayled vp the riuer till we came to *Heron* Ilands, so called from the infinite number of that fowle there. The first of those Ilands, wee called Saint *Clements*; The second, Saint *Katharines*; And the third, Saint *Cecilies*. Wee tooke land first in Saint *Clements*, which is compassed about with a shallow water, and admitts no accesse without wading; here, by the ouerturning of the Shallop, the maids which had beene washing at the land, were almost drowned, beside the losse of much linnen, and amongst the rest I lost the best of mine, which is a very maine losse in these parts.

The

(3.)

The ground is couered thicke with pokickeries (which is a wild Wall-nut, very hard and thick of shell; but the meate (though little) is passing sweete) with black Wall-nuts, and acrons bigger then ours. It abounds with Vines, and salletts, hearbs, and flowers, full of Cedar, and sassafras. It is but 400 acres bigg, and therefore too little for vs to settle vpon.

Heere wee went to a place, where a large tree was made into a Crosse; and taking it on our shoulders, wee carried it to the place appointed for it. The Gouernour and Commissioners putting their hands first vnto it, then the rest of the chiefest aduenturers. At the place prepared wee all kneeled downe, and said certaine Prayers; taking possession of this Countrey for our Sauiour; and for our soueraigne Lord the King of *England*.

Here our gouernour had good aduice giuen him, not to land for good and all, before hee had beene with the Emperour of *Paschattoway*, and had declared vnto him the cause of our comming: which was, first to learne them a diuine Doctrine, which would lead their soules to a place of happinesse after this life were ended: And also to enrich them with such ornaments of a ciuill life, wherewith our Countrey doth abound: and this Emperour being satisfied, none of the inferiour Kings would stirre. In conformity to this aduice, hee tooke two Pinnaces, his owne, and another hired at *Virginia*; and leauing the ship before Saint *Clements* at Anchor, went vp the riuer, and landing on the south-side, and finding the *Indians* fled for feare, came to *Patoemeck* Towne, where the King being a child, *Archihau* his Vncle gouerned both him, and his Countrey for him. Hee gaue all the company good wellcome; and one of the company hauing entred into a little discourse with him touching the errours of their religion, hee seemed well pleased therewith; and at his going away desired him to returne vnto him againe, telling him hee should liue at his Table, his men should hunt for him, and hee would diuide all with him.

From hence they went to *Paschattoway*. All were heere armed: 500 Bow-men came to the Water-side. The Emperour himselfe more fearelesse then the rest, came priuately a boord, where hee was courteously entertained; and vnderstanding wee came in a peaceable manner, bade vs welcome, and gaue vs leaue to sit downe in

A 3   what

IV.2. Only three copies have survived of Father Andrew White's *Relation of the Successefull Beginnings of the Lord Baltemore's Plantation in Mary-land* (London, 1634), which is depicted here. In the original Latin version of this account, the highlighted paragraph began as follows: "On the day of the Annunciation of the Most Holy Virgin Mary in the year 1634, we celebrated the Mass for the first time on this island. This had never been done before in this part of the world."

of the sacrament in detail to his Jesuit superiors in Rome, the version of this journey published for the English public judiciously deleted all reference to it. In Protestant England it was always wise not to mention the "papists" in Maryland (figure IV.2.).

The situation for Catholics in Maryland certainly represented an improvement over England, but there were problems in Lord Baltimore's colony nonetheless. Catholics never constituted a majority of the population and were cautioned to exercise discretion in their worship and in their religious discussions. For two short periods in the 1640s and 1650s Lord Baltimore lost control of the colony to a group of Puritans who seized the opportunity to persecute the colony's Catholics. Plagued by a shortage of priests and completely cut off from the Church hierarchy, Maryland's Catholics suffered from many of the same difficulties that beset the Church of England in neighboring Virginia.

Still, Maryland represented the only legitimate opportunity for a Roman Catholic community to develop in the English colonies. Even tolerant Rhode Island granted civil rights specifically to *Protestant* males, excluding Roman Catholics from participating in the colony's political affairs. Not until the Revolu-

61

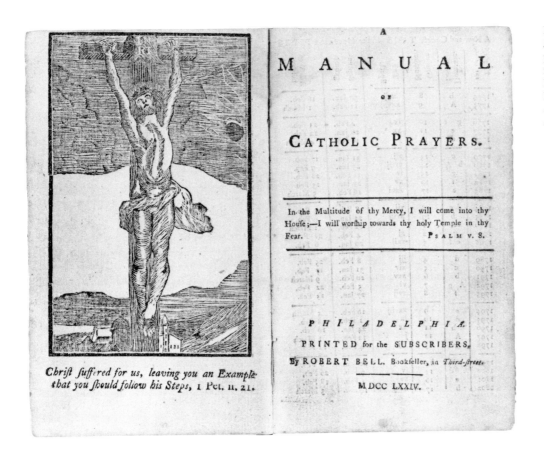

IV.3. This *Manual of Catholic Prayers*, published in Philadelphia in 1774, was compiled to meet the needs of a growing Roman Catholic population in Pennsylvania. It is one of the earliest Roman Catholic publications in the English colonies.

tionary War brought a large number of French Catholic soldiers to the colony was a Catholic mass said openly. In 1783, when some of these Frenchmen decided to stay, the Rhode Island legislature passed a law extending the rights that had been granted to Protestants in 1663 to Roman Catholics.

It is possible that in Rhode Island, as in other colonies, a few Catholics lived quietly without the benefit of the ministrations of the Church. But with the exception of Maryland, and eventually Pennsylvania (figure IV.3.), it was well past the end of the colonial period before Roman Catholic communities flourished anywhere in Anglo-America.

48
Andrew White, S.J. (1579–1656).
A Relation of the Successeful Beginnings of the Lord Baltemore's Plantation in Maryland.
([London], 1634)

The popularity of Stuart rule in England was hardly enhanced by the fact that various Stuart kings favored Catholicism or their Catholic subjects. Lord Baltimore was one Catholic so favored when Charles I granted him the colony of Maryland in 1632. The colony offered a haven for England's Catholics as well as a business opportunity for Baltimore. Because English public opinion was so staunchly anti-Catholic, the religious element in this colonization venture had to be underplayed. This account of the arrival of the first settlers was written by a Jesuit priest, Andrew White, who participated in the venture and celebrated the first mass on Maryland's shores. White's detailed report written for his superiors in Rome was replete with references to holy days, angels, and the first mass. This translation was revised for English audiences, and all overtly Roman Catholic references were deleted. Holy Mass became, in this account, "wee all kneeled down and said certaine Prayers." White was free to say no more in England (figure IV.2.).

49

A Moderate and Safe Expedient.
([London], 1646)

During the years of the English civil war there was more open discussion on a wide variety of subjects than ever before in English history. Although the religious ferment of the era was overwhelmingly Protestant, at least one pamphleteer felt free to come forward to advocate the cause of the country's Catholics. *A Moderate and Safe Expedient* suggested that Catholics be tolerated in England or else be encouraged to remove to Maryland.

50

John Langford.
A Just and Cleere Refutation.
(London, 1655)

Maryland's famous Act Concerning Religion was first published in this 1655 pamphlet by John Langford. The law allowed liberty of conscience for all Christians, which was the only way Catholics could be granted religious freedom in an English colony. The act did prohibit certain heresies, but the objectionable beliefs did not include any of those held by Catholics. The act also prohibited name-calling in an effort to reduce animosities. Despite such efforts to assure liberty to Catholics, the religious history of Maryland was marked by factionalism and strife, and the colony's Puritans took every opportunity to seize control and persecute Catholics. Maryland's liberty of conscience, pragmatically rather than ideologically based, was never very successful.

51

Calendrier Français.
(Newport, [1780])

Although today Rhode Island has the largest percentage of Catholics of any state in the United States, its Catholic population dates back only to the late colonial period. The French came to Rhode Island during the Revolution, and a number of soldiers decided to remain after the war was over. While the French army was still here, the French fleet press printed French-language works for the use of the troops. This calendar, now rare, was one of the works printed on that press.

Jews

Like Roman Catholicism, contemporary American Judaism owes more to nineteenth-century immigration than to the colonial past. Yet Jews had settled in the region that would become the United States as early as 1654.

The first Jewish community came to New Amsterdam, a Dutch town in New Netherlands (later New York), from Recife in eastern Brazil. They were Sephardic Jews who had left Spain or Portugal after being expelled from the Iberian peninsula during the 1490s. Many of the Sephardic Jews went to Holland, which was the most tolerant European country during this era. When the Dutch took Recife from Portugal in 1630, a group of Jews joined in the colonization effort there. Those who came to the Dutch colony of New Amsterdam established the congregation Shearith Israel (meaning "Remnant of Israel").

By the end of the colonial period there were six separate Jewish communities in British North America, and additional congregations had been established in Charleston, Savannah, Richmond, Philadelphia, and Newport. These communities were predominantly Sephardic. The Charleston congregation was the largest, numbering more than four hundred people. The group that settled in Newport, Rhode Island, had come from Holland in 1658. Although their history is not well documented for the early years, we do know that fifteen Jewish families purchased a plot for a burial ground in 1677. An influx of settlers from the Dutch West Indian island of Curaçao augmented the congregation during the 1730s and 1740s. Although they were not completely accepted even in that relatively tolerant colony, their numbers grew, and in 1762 they were able to build the beautiful Touro Synagogue (figure IV.4.).

Like Anglicans and Catholics, American Jews had to manage without the spiritual leadership they were accustomed to in Europe. There were no rabbis in residence in the colonies, so cantors took on more responsibilities. In 1773 Rabbi Raphael Haim Isaac Carigal, a rabbi from Palestine, toured Philadelphia, New York, and Newport visiting the Jewish communities in each of these three cities. One of the sermons he preached in Newport–"The Salvation of Israel"– was published; it was the first publication of its kind in the North American colonies.

Roman Catholics and Jews were the only non-Protestant Europeans in the English colonies. As such, they constituted a very distinct minority. Yet Protestants often differed greatly among themselves as well. Denominational and ethnic variations within a broad Protestant spectrum contributed to still greater religious diversity within the colonies. By the eve of the American Revolution, the entire range of European religion was re-created in the colonies, without the national boundaries of European establishments.

IV.4. Touro Synagogue in Newport, Rhode Island, designed by Peter Harrison and constructed in 1762, is the only surviving synagogue built in colonial British America. Aside from its importance to the history of religion, it is considered an architectural classic. This photograph, taken in ca. 1909, was provided by the Rhode Island Historical Society.

52
Isaac Pinto, (1720–1791) translator.
Prayers for Shabbath, Rosh-Hashanah, and Kippur.
([New York], 1766)

The oldest Jewish community in British North America was the New York City congregation of Sephardic Jews. After more than a century in an English colony, they felt the need for an English-language translation of Hebrew prayers. In 1766 one of their number, Issac Pinto, published this work, which was "according to the Order of the Spanish and Portuguese Jews."

53
Haim Isaac Carigal (1733–1777).
A Sermon Preached at the Synagogue, in Newport, Rhode Island, called "The Salvation of Israel."
(Newport, 1773)

Rabbi Carigal was a Palestinian-born Jew who traveled extensively through the Orient and Europe before coming to the colonies in 1773. He spent five months in Philadelphia, New York, and Newport, visiting his co-religionists in each town. During his stay in Rhode Island he formed a lasting friendship with the Congregational minister Ezra Stiles, who eventually became president of Yale College. Stiles was an avid student of Hebrew and corresponded with Carigal in later years. This sermon, preached in Newport by Carigal, was translated by Abraham Lopez.

54
Judah Monis (1683–1764).
*Dickdook Leshon Gnebreet: A Grammar of
the Hebrew Tongue.*
(Boston, 1735)

This book, the first Hebrew grammar published in North America, was intended for use by Harvard College students who were required to learn Hebrew in preparation for careers as ministers. Judah Monis, the author, was the first Jew to receive a Harvard degree and the first instructor in Hebrew employed by the college. In 1722, two years after receiving his degree, Monis converted to Christianity and was baptized at College Hall. He continued to observe the seventh day (Saturday) as the Sabbath after his conversion, however. Eventually, Monis, who married a Christian, became a full member of the First Church in Cambridge.

55
Increase Mather (1639–1723).
*A Dissertation Concerning the Future
Conversion of the Jewish Nation.*
(London, 1709)

Like many other Protestant scholars, the Boston minister Increase Mather believed that the Day of Judgment was close at hand. The Book of Revelation had convinced many people that Jews would convert to Christianity in large numbers just before the end of the world. In 1709 Mather published his ideas on this topic, which was of great interest to a scholarly English audience. Through their studies of ancient Jewish history and speculations such as these, English Protestants displayed a special interest in Judaism and the Jewish people. Even though they considered the conversion of the Jews desirable, they generally approved of them more, or at least feared them less, than Roman Catholics.

Presbyterians

Presbyterianism was a branch of European Protestantism theologically quite similar to English Congregationalism. Presbyterians disagreed with their Congregational brethren, though, on church organization, favoring a system of presbyteries instead of congregational autonomy. These presbyteries—or governing bodies—issued declarations about faith and practice which members were expected to follow. Though the Presbyterians in England participated in the Puritan movement, they were the most conservative of the Protestant dissenters in both their religious and social views; some Anglicans even advocated expanding the Church of England to include or "comprehend" them after the Restoration.

The Presbyterians in the colonies, however, were most often people of non-English backgrounds. A number of European nations—including Holland, some German states, and most notably, Scotland—had adopted the presbyterian system when they organized their national churches. The Dutch, German, and Scottish immigrants who adhered to the "Reformed" religion of their homeland were all Presbyterians in essence, but, despite their similar beliefs, they considered themselves members of different churches.

The history of the Dutch Reformed Church in America was somewhat unusual, for the adherents of that faith had been conquered by the English. Most non-English groups had migrated to colonies already under English control, but the Dutch were already settled in New Netherlands when the English seized it in 1664, renaming it New York. New Netherlands was sparsely peopled at the time of the British takeover, having only about eight thousand inhabitants. Like the English in Virginia, the Dutch had not been entirely successful in transferring their established church to the New World. Just as Virginia's Anglicans remained under the jurisdiction of the Bishop of London, so the Dutch Reformed Church retained its ties to the Amsterdam presbytery until late in the colonial period.

The Dutch settlers were not particularly happy to fall under English rule, but they were at least allowed to continue to practice their religion. Despite a shortage of ministers and a dearth of well-organized congregations, the Dutch Reformed Church continued to be active in New York and the neighboring colonies throughout the colonial era.

A second group of Presbyterians came to the colonies from Scotland. The founder of the Scottish church, John Knox (ca. 1513–1573), was greatly influenced by John Calvin (1509–1564). During the sixteenth century Knox organized Scotland into presbyteries, creating a national church along reformed lines. Later, the Scottish army played a leading role during the English civil war, supporting the Puritans in Parliament against the King. Thus the kinship between English dissenters and Scots Presbyterians was strong.

During the seventeenth century the scattered migration by Scottish and Scots-Irish Presbyterians did not lead to the development of autonomous Presbyterian churches. The early eighteenth century, however, saw the establishment of separate presbyteries and the growth of a largely Scots-Irish Presbyterian community in the colonies. The Scots-Irish were Scottish Protestants encouraged by Oliver Cromwell to settle in Ireland in the 1650s, with the aim of spreading Protestantism to that Catholic country. Then as now, the Protestants in Ireland were an unpopular minority, and many chose to emigrate to America rather than to stay in Ireland. For the most part, these people settled in the middle colonies, expanding the number of presbyteries there from one, in 1706, to three in 1716 (figure IV.5.). In Pennsylvania they constituted a large non-Quaker minority. By the Revolutionary period they had come to dominate not only the frontier of Pennsylvania, but that of most southern colonies as well.

56
Westminster Assembly of Divines
(1643–1645).
The Shorter Catechism.
(Boston, 1683)

During the 1640s a group of leading Puritan ministers met at Westminster, England, to prepare a confession of faith, a catechism, and other theological instruments. At the time, Parliament had seized control of England and planned to institute a Presby-

terian national church in place of the Church of England. This plan failed, but the work of the Westminster Assembly of Divines provided important guidelines for Scottish and English Puritans to use in the future. This was the first American printing of the catechism developed by the Assembly, published for use by the British Calvinists in the colonies.

57
Dutch Reformed Church.
The Heidelbergh Catechism or Method of
Instruction in the Christian Religion.
([New York, 1767])

The Heidelbergh Catechism, originally prepared in 1563, was the original catechism used by the Dutch Reformed Church

in America. In 1767 an English translation was deemed necessary because few adherents of the church still spoke Dutch. It was bound with a translation of the *Psalms of David* which had been set to the music used in the Dutch church.

58
George Scot (d. 1685).
The Model of the Government of the
Province of East-New-Jersey.
(Edinburgh, 1685)

While West New Jersey was settled largely by Quakers, East New Jersey's population was predominantly Calvinist, either Con-

gregational or Presbyterian. George Scot wrote this pamphlet to publicize the colony to Scots men and women who might be interested in settling there. In it, he reprinted the letter of an indentured servant that described the religious composition of the colony.

IV.5. The experience of the
Scots-Irish Presbyterian minister Francis Makemie, who
was imprisoned in New York
for preaching without a license,
was characteristic of an era
when civil authorities attempted to control the exercise of
religion.

A
NARRATIVE
Of a New and Unusual
AMERICAN
Imprisonment
Of Two
PRESBYTERIAN MINISTERS :
And Profecution of
Mr. Francis Makemie

One of them, for Preaching one SERMON
at the City of NEW-YORK.

By a Learner of Law, and Lover of Liberty.

Printed for the Publisher. 1707.

59
Francis Makemie (1658–1708).
*A Narrative of a New and Unusual
American Imprisonment of Two
Presbyterian Ministers.*
([New York], 1707)

Francis Makemie was a Scots-Irish Presbyterian minister who preached in the colonies from 1681 until his death. He led the
group of ministers who met in Philadelphia
to establish the first American presbytery.

The next year he was imprisoned and fined
for preaching in New York without a
license. When he appealed his case, he
was acquitted. The legislature further passed an act ending this sort of persecution,
which was one landmark on the road to
religious liberty. Makemie issued this
anonymous pamphlet about the incident in
an effort to bring adverse publicity to such
persecution (figure IV.5.).

The third group of Presbyterians in North America was the German Reformed church. In the eighteenth century the German-speaking area of Europe
was divided into a few hundred separate political entities. The established
churches in the northern states were either Lutheran or German Reformed.
Decades of devastating wars throughout central Europe drove many people
from their homelands. By the early eighteenth century numerous adherents of
the German Reformed church were migrating to the middle colonies. Those
who came to New York were usually incorporated into the Dutch Reformed
Church, but the settlers in Pennsylvania were forced to organize new churches.

The first congregation in Pennsylvania was gathered in 1719, but the German
Reformed Church did not have enough strength to support a yearly gathering
of its American church leaders for another thirty years. By that time the Dutch
Reformed Church, older and better established, had come to exert a considerable amount of authority over the German churches. Finally, in the 1790s, the

German congregations declared themselves fully independent of Dutch control, and established a separate synod to oversee their affairs.

These German, Dutch, Scottish, and Scots-Irish settlers, while all "Presbyterians" in their church polity and theology, owed allegiance to culturally distinct churches in Europe. Their disparate ethnic origins lent a greater variety to the religious scene in America than their common commitment to Presbyterianism would suggest.

60
Congregation of God in the Spirit.
Kurzer Catechismus vor etliche Gemeinen Jesu aus der Reformirten Religion in Pennsylvania, die sich zum alten Berner Synodo halten: herausgegeben von Johannes Bechtel, Diener des Worts Gottes.
(Philadelphia, 1742)

This catechism was compiled by Johannes Bechtel, pastor of a congregation in Germantown, and N. L. Graf von Zinzendorf and published for use by the expanding

German Reformed Church in Pennsylvania. Benjamin Franklin, who was on very good terms with the various ethnic groups in the colony, printed the volume.

French Huguenots

The French Huguenots, although they had little lasting impact on the English colonies as a group, made significant individual contributions to colonial life for a number of years after 1685. Huguenots were French Protestants who, by the 1598 Edict of Nantes, had been granted freedom to worship in their native country. In 1685, however, the Edict was revoked, resulting in the departure of some 300,000 French Protestants who chose to leave their homeland rather than accept Catholicism, as most of their community did. Many traveled to England where they were encouraged to settle in the colonies.

A group of Huguenots established a church at Narragansett in Rhode Island in 1686, but conflicts over land rights impelled these French settlers to move on. Huguenot churches were also founded in other colonies, including the Carolinas, Virginia, New York, and Massachusetts. The Huguenots gradually lost their ethnic distinctiveness, blending into the general population (figure IV.6.). Many found the Anglican Church especially appealing on social grounds, and chose to join it. Only for a short time before the turn of the century did Huguenots flourish as a distinct group.

61
Durand of Dauphiné (fl. 1685–1687).
Voyages D'Un François, Exilé pour la Religion.
(Hague, 1687)

A Huguenot named Durand traveled in the colonies after the revocation of the Edict of Nantes forced him to leave his native France. This account of his journey included many observations about the relative merits of various colonies for settlement by Huguenots. The governor of Virginia reportedly told Monsieur Durand that his co-religionists ought to settle in

Virginia. Colonies further north would prove too cold and the Carolinas too hot for the French constitution; thus, he argued, Virginia's climate was the most appealing. Durand further claimed that the governor was prepared to offer religious sanctuary to Huguenots, whose Protestantism was quite similar to that of the established church in Virginia. Many Huguenots did eventually join Anglican churches and some chose to settle in Virginia.

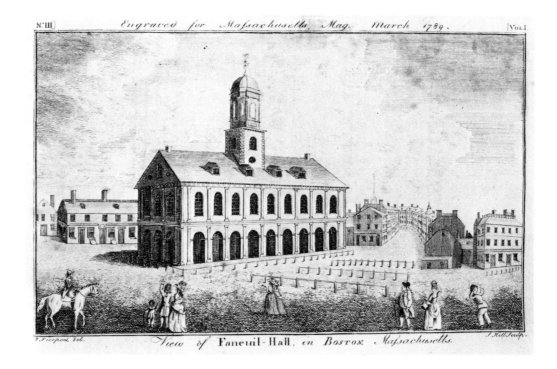

IV.6. Faneuil Hall in Boston, as depicted in 1789 in the *Massachusetts Magazine*, volume I, number 3. The hall was given to the town of Boston by Peter Faneuil, a Huguenot merchant who immigrated to Massachusetts. The hall's subsequent importance as a community center is symbolic of the ease with which the Huguenots were assimilated into colonial life.

Lutherans

As with members of the Reformed churches and Presbyterians, the Lutherans in the colonies came from at least three different European countries. Martin Luther (1483–1546), the great leader of the Protestant Reformation, was a German Catholic priest when he launched his critique of the Church. Throughout his life, Luther claimed to be working for the reformation of the Roman Catholic church rather than for the creation of a new denomination. It was only after his death that Lutheran churches were officially established. Subsequently, these churches came to dominate north central Europe.

The first Lutheran churches in North America were founded by the Swedes who mounted a modest and short-lived colonization venture on the banks of the Delaware River from 1638 to 1655. First the Dutch and later the English took control of the area, abruptly ending Swedish imperial plans for the region. Still, these Swedish Lutheran churches remained and were able to retain their separate identity throughout most of the colonial period. One of the Swedish ministers translated Luther's catechism into the Delaware Indian tongue; this was the first Christian document produced in a North American Indian language (figure IV.7.).

Lutherans also came to the colonies from Holland and Germany. Two Dutch Lutheran churches were already established in New Netherlands when it was seized by the English in 1664. Early in the next century, German-speaking Lutherans began arriving in New York and Pennsylvania. This group eventually came to dominate colonial American Lutheranism.

The Lutheran churches, like so many other colonial religious groups, suffered from being cut off from all the amenities of its parent religious organization in Europe. In the 1740s a brilliant German Lutheran minister, Henry Melchior Muhlenberg, was sent to the colonies by church leaders living in London during the reign of King George II. Muhlenberg labored for more than forty years to organize the Lutheran churches, leaving a voluminous journal recounting his efforts and a securely established religious organization (figure IV.8.). By the time of the American Revolution there were more than eighty Lutheran congregations in Pennsylvania, New York, Virginia, and North Carolina. The Lutherans, whether of German, Dutch, or Swedish origin, constituted a further variation in the spectrum of European Protestantism in the English-controlled colonies of North America.

IV.7. The frontispiece from John Campanius's Swedish-Algonquian catechism, published in Stockholm in 1696. Campanius was a missionary in New Sweden from 1642 to 1648, where he learned enough of the Delaware language to prepare this translation, with commentary, of Luther's catechism. The work may be compared to John Eliot's Indian Bible and Roger Williams's *A Key into the Language of America* as an early example of the translation of Christian doctrine into the languages of the North American Indians.

62
Johannes Campanius, Holmiensis (1601–1683), translator.
Lutheri Catechismus, Öfwersatt på American-Virginiske Språket.
(Stockholm, 1696)

Johannes Campanius, the most noteworthy Swedish Lutheran minister in America, translated Luther's catechism into the Delaware Indian language. His *Catechismus* remained in manuscript until the 1690s, when the Swedish king took a new interest in these churches, which had come under English rule. Campanius's translation was published in Stockholm at royal expense in 1696, and five hundred copies were sent to the colonies to be used for converting the Indians (figure IV.7.).

Heinr. Melch. Mühlenberg, der heil. Schrift Doctor und des Evang. luth. Minist. Senior.

geb. d. 6 Sept. 1711 gest. d. 7 Octob. 1787

63
Just Heinrich Christian Helmuth
(1745–1825).
Denkmal der Liebe und Achtung Welches seiner Hochwürden dem Herrn D. Heinrich Melchior Mühlenberg... ist gesetzet worden.
(Philadelphia, 1788)

This memorial was written to commemorate the life of Heinrich Melchior Muhlenberg (1711–1787). Muhlenberg was born in Hanover (now part of Germany), received a university education, and was ordained in 1739. From 1742 until his death he worked to unite and expand the Lutheran church in America. He formed the Pennsylvania Ministerium, which served much like a presbytery for the Lutheran churches. He also worked with the leaders of the Swedish churches to bring order to American Lutheranism, and laid the groundwork for the modern church in the United States (figure IV.8.).

German Pietist Sects

The German-speaking area of Europe, although predominantly Protestant, encompassed wide variations in theological principles, most of which were to take root in the North American colonies. German Presbyterians and Lutherans were not the only ones to emigrate; so did adherents of a number of "Pietist" sects. Most of these sects advocated believer's baptism and had a strikingly mystical bent (figure IV.9.). Pietists often settled in Pennsylvania, a place they found appealing because of the promise of religious liberty, the availability of land for settlement, and perhaps the kindred mysticism of the Quakers.

The first of these Pietist groups to settle in America were the Mennonite Anabaptists, who came to Pennsylvania just as that colony was being established. They settled throughout rural Pennsylvania and were later joined by a more conservative Mennonite group called the Amish. The Amish are famous today for continuing to adhere to an ascetic style of life.

A second group of German Anabaptists, the Church of the Brethren, or "Dunkers," came to Pennsylvania during the 1720s. Dunker elder Christoph

IV.9. Pietistic sects often participated in such symbolic recreations of biblical events as the footwashing depicted here, from David Cranz's history of the Moravian Brethren, *Kurze, zuverlässige Nachricht von der, unter dem Namen der Böhmisch-Mährischen Brüder bekanten, Kirche Unitas Fratrum* (1757).

IV.10. Baptism of American Indians by Moravian priests, also from David Cranz's *Kurze, zuverlässige Nachricht* (see figure IV.9.).

Saur produced the first Western-language translation of the Bible printed in America, his German Bible, in 1743. Some of the Dunkers, led by Conrad Beissell (1691–1768), withdrew into a semi-monastic community called the Ephrata Cloister. The Ephrata brethren, more extreme than the Dunkers generally, practiced faith healing, a seventh-day Sabbath, and separation of the sexes. The Ephrata branch disbanded before the Revolution, but a small number of Dunkers continued their religious practice into the nineteenth century.

A third German sect, the Moravians (or Unitas Fratrum), settled in the English colonies for the specific purpose of evangelizing among the Native Americans. Again, some of their most significant settlements were in the colony of Pennsylvania, which was developing a large non-English population. They also settled in North Carolina at Winston-Salem. This town, along with Nazareth and Bethlehem in Pennsylvania, was founded as a semi-communal colony where farming and crafts produced a profit that supported Moravian missionary efforts. These efforts were ultimately hampered by the continued hostilities between the Indians and European colonists, but of all the religious communities, the Moravians made the most extensive attempt at missionizing the Native Americans (figure IV.10.).

Thus, various German sectarian groups, united by some similar beliefs and common language but divided into separate religious entities, came to the English colonies after 1680. Concentrated in Pennsylvania, they also established a few settlements in the southern and other middle colonies. Although the German pietist belief in adult baptism was shared by the growing number of English-speaking Baptists, no attempt was ever made to unite English and German Baptists. In the 1740s the Moravians attempted to bring all the German Baptists into one sect, but the effort failed, and the German sects continued as separate groups throughout the colonial period.

64
Christoph Saur (1693–1758), publisher and printer.
Biblia, das ist: Die Heilige Schrift Altes und Neues Testaments.
(Germantown, Pennsylvania, 1743)

Christoph Saur, a member of the German sect known as the Dunkers, became a famous publisher and bookseller in America. The type for this Bible had to be brought from Frankfurt, but Saur eventually assembled craftsmen in Germantown who could make paper, ink, and type. This was the first Bible printed in a European language in the colonies. Earlier, Christians in North America had relied on Bibles imported from Europe.

65
Paradisisches Wunder-Spiel.
(Ephrata, Pennsylvania, 1767)

This collection of spiritual music was prepared for the use of the Ephrata community in Pennsylvania. An offshoot of the Dunkers, the Ephrata brethren were founded by Conrad Beissel. They placed great emphasis on music in their semi-cloistered community, and published numerous collections of this sort.

66
Congregation of God in the Spirit.
Extract aus des Conferenz-Schreibers Johann Jacob Müllers Registratur von der sechsten Versammlung der evangelischen Arbeiter in Pennsylvania.
([Philadelphia, 1742])

The Moravians were active missionaries to the American Indians. This work reported on a conference held in Pennsylvania to review their evangelical efforts in that colony.

Afro-Americans

As with other aspects of the history of Afro-Americans, the course of black American religion has unique characteristics. Late in the seventeenth century the English followed the example of the European colonizers of South America and the West Indies and began importing Africans in large numbers to work as slaves. The slaves were forced to travel either directly from Africa to North American ports, or through the West Indies to the continental settlements.

A few of these slaves were Muslims, but the vast majority adhered to traditional West African religions (figure IV.11.). The life of a slave was not conducive to maintaining these traditional faiths. Differences in language and belief among slaves made worshipping together difficult, and in any case slave-owners discouraged private meetings of large numbers of slaves. In some areas, however, such as the Georgia Sea Islands, a striking number of traditional African beliefs and practices persisted well into the nineteenth century. In many other places, they probably survived in only a limited way.

Only gradually did Christianity become a part of black American life. The rate at which it did so was determined by demographic factors and conditions of servitude. In the northern colonies, where blacks were few, they were generally included in the local Christian community from the outset.

Boston, as an urban seaport, had a larger slave population than was typical of New England generally. Like all other residents of the colony, slaves were required by law to attend church services. In order to better meet the spiritual needs of the Boston black community, the minister Cotton Mather organized a Society for Negroes in 1693. The group met on Sunday evenings to hear a sermon, learn prayers, and recite catechisms.

In the next century the black poet Phillis Wheatley was a member of one of the Boston congregations, as well as the slave of a prosperous tailor in that town (figure IV.12.). Her poetry revealed that the young slave could be well versed in Christianity. This fact made her a popular symbol for whites who hoped to see all the blacks in America, and eventually all of Africa, Christianized.

67
Olaudah Equiano (b. 1745).
The Interesting Narrative of the Life of Olaudah Equiano, or Gustavus Vassa, the African, Written by Himself.
(New York, 1791)

An Ibo from the area of present-day Nigeria, Olaudah Equiano was shipped to Barbados as a boy to be sold as a slave. He was found physically unacceptable for the grueling labor that slaves on West Indian sugar plantations had to perform, and was therefore sold instead in Virginia. This narrative was written much later, after he had become a Christian and regained his freedom. It was published first in England and later in the United States as part of the anti-slavery movement. Equiano's obvious intelligence and his fervent Christianity were offered as proof that slavery was a degrading and unjust institution. Though the author stressed his own conversion, he also remembered the traditional beliefs of his boyhood among the Ibo. Many other slaves who left no written record recalled such beliefs, which formed the basis of African religious derivatives in America (figure IV.11.).

68
Phillis [Wheatley] (ca. 1753–1784).
An Elegiac Poem on the Death of that Celebrated Divine and Eminent Servant of Jesus Christ, the Reverend and Learned George Whitefield.
(Boston, [1770])

Famous as the "African poetess," Phillis was the seventeen-year old slave of John Wheatley when she wrote this poem. Brought to the colonies just nine years earlier, she had learned English and converted to Christianity under the tutelage of her mistress, who eventually freed her. Many of her poems were religious in nature. The subject of this poem was the famous evangelist George Whitefield, who toured the American colonies repeatedly after 1739, and converted many (figure IV.12.).

IV.11. The frontispiece of *The Interesting Narrative of the Life of Olaudah Equiano or Gustavus Vassa, the African, Written by Himself* (New York, 1791).

IV.12. The frontispiece of Phillis Wheatley's *Poems on Various Subjects* (Published in London: sold in Boston, 1773). (See also figure V.2.).

69
Ezra Stiles (1727–1795) and Samuel Hopkins (1721–1803).
To the Public.
([Newport, 1776])

When this work was published, the two Newport ministers who were its authors had been involved for quite a while in a plan to send two black missionaries back to Africa. This pamphlet contained their proposal to raise money to buy the freedom of one of the men, to finance the edu-

cation of both, and to send them to Africa. Some money had already been raised when the proposal circulated in manuscript. *To the Public* both reached out to a larger audience and reported what had been done with the contributions received so far. The pamphlet also reprinted a letter from Phillis Wheatley to the two men who were being trained to serve as missionaries.

With this end in mind, two Rhode Island ministers, Ezra Stiles and Samuel Hopkins, initiated a campaign to raise money for the education of two African men, Bristol Yamma and John Quamine, who were expected to return to Africa as free men and missionaries. Yamma and Quamine had been slaves and members of the Newport Congregational Church when they were recruited for this project. Their case and that of Wheatley indicated the potential for the integration of blacks living in New England into the white Christian community.

In the South, where slaves were more numerous and white fears of insurrection more intense, the situation for blacks was quite different. Many masters were hesitant to have their slaves baptized for fear that this would end their servitude, the idea being that a fellow Christian could not be held in bondage. By 1706 at least six colonies had passed laws stipulating that baptism did not alter a slave's temporal status. Even this measure did not end white fears about Christianizing slaves. Many people suspected that Christianity, with its message of equality and brotherhood, would make slaves less subservient. Furthermore, with clergy in short supply throughout the southern colonies, any serious effort to catechize slaves would have to be undertaken at the expense of the education of white parishioners.

It was not until dissenting ministers began touring the southern colonies later in the eighteenth century that southern blacks converted to Christianity in substantial numbers. Anglican plantation owners looked askance at revival meetings that brought together blacks and whites in an emotional outpouring of religious fervor. Presbyterians, Baptists, and later Methodists all successfully proselytized among slaves and free blacks. The uniqueness of modern Southern evangelical styles owes a great deal to the traditions and needs brought into the churches by these converts.

After the Revolution, black Americans would establish separate congregations and even some new denominations, but during the colonial era blacks were included in white-dominated churches throughout the colonies. Within these churches, they developed their own faith and traditions, which would provide the foundations for the all-black churches of later years.

(32)

preach near the house, under the shade of some large trees. But the rain made it impracticable. The house was greatly crouded, and four or five hundred stood at the doors and windows, and listened with unabated attention. I preached from *Ezekiel*'s vision of the *dry bones*. *And there was a great shaking.* I was obliged to stop again and again, and beg of the people to compose themselves. But they could not: Some on their knees, and some on their faces, were crying mightily to God all the time I was preaching. Hundreds of Negroes were among them, with the tears streaming down their black faces. The same power we found in meeting the Society, and many were enabled to rejoice with joy unspeakable. In the cool of the Evening I preached out of doors, and many found an uncommon blessing.

Every day in the ensuing week I preached to large and attentive congregations. Indeed the weather was violently hot, and the fatigue of riding and preaching so often was great. But God made up all this to me, by his comfortable presence. *Thursday*, 11. I preached to a large congregation, at the Preaching-house near Mr. *Jarratt*'s. After preaching at several places on Friday and Saturday, on *Sunday*, 14. I came to Mr. *Boshcua*'s, where I preached and met the Society. The congregation was, as before, abundantly larger than the Chapel could contain. And we had almost such a day as fourteen days ago: only attended with a more deep and solemn work. What a work is God working in this

(33)

this corner of Mr. *Jarratt*'s Parish! It seemed as if all the Country, for nine or ten miles round, were ready to turn to God.

In the Evening I rode to Mr. *Smith*'s, and found a whole Family fearing and loving God. Mr. *Smith*, a sensible and judicious man, had been for many years a Justice of the Peace. By hearing the truth as it is in Jesus, he and his wife first, and then all his children had attained that peace that passeth all understanding. He observed, "How amazing the Change was, which had been lately wrought in the place where he lived! That before the Methodists came into these parts, when he was called by his office to attend the Court, there was nothing but Drunkenness, Cursing, Swearing, and Fighting, most of the time the Court sat: Whereas now nothing is heard but Prayer and Praise, and conversing about God, and the things of God."

Monday 15. I rode towards *North Carolina*. In every place the Congregations were large, and received the word with all readiness of mind. I know not that I have spent such a week since I came to *America*. I saw every where such a simplicity in the people, with such a vehement thirst after the word of God, that I frequently preached and continued in prayer, till I was hardly able to stand. Indeed there was no getting away from them, while I was able to speak one sentence for God.

Sunday 21. I preached at *Ronoaky* Chapel to more than double of what the House would contain. In general,

IV.13. From *A Brief Narrative of the Revival of Religion in Virginia.* 3d edition (London, 1778), attributed to Devereux Jarratt.

70
Samuel Davies (1723–1761).
Letters from the Rev. Samuel Davies, etc.
shewing the State of Religion in Virginia,
particularly among the Negroes.
(London, 1757)

Davies, a Presbyterian minister, was born
in Delaware and educated in Pennsylvania.
He was sent by the New York synod to
minister to a newly gathered church in
Hanover County, Virginia. The most important of the growing number of dissenting
ministers in that colony, Davies battled
with authorities for a license to preach
and, in effect, to win toleration for all dissenters there. He also helped to raise
money to found the College of New Jersey
(later Princeton), and served as its president from 1759 to 1761. Davies worked to
establish the first presbytery in Virginia
and took an active part in the religious
education of blacks.

71
Devereux Jarratt (1733–1801).
A Brief Narrative of the Revival of Religion
in Virginia.
(London, 1778)

This pamphlet, probably written by
Devereux Jarratt, contained letters by various clergymen touching on the religious
revivals that swept many southern blacks
into Christian churches. Such eyewitness
reports were eagerly awaited by interested
English audiences (figure IV.13.).

We usually think of the North American colonies that became the United States
as being English and Protestant. In terms of both political control and numerical
superiority, that picture is accurate. But collectively the non-English and non-
Protestant inhabitants formed a substantial minority. For example, in Pennsylvania, where the Quakers' liberal religious policies and the continued availability of land attracted many settlers, the English Friends were eventually
overwhelmed by other groups. In South Carolina, the English colonists were
temporarily outnumbered by the Africans they imported in large numbers.

Even though English Protestants dominated almost everywhere, other
groups often added a distinctly different religious, ethnic, and cultural dimen-
sion. Those areas that were predominantly English and Protestant, particularly
New England, were settled early and relatively densely by the English. There
the variations tended to be within Protestantism, as was largely the case in
Rhode Island (with the exception of the Jewish community in Newport). But
in the middle and southern colonies, English conquest (as of the Dutch or the
Swedes), enslavement (as of the Africans), or immigration (Germans, French,
Scots, or Scots-Irish) added a religious diversity that was also cultural.

By the middle of the eighteenth century the colonies England controlled
had, in a haphazard and largely unintended way, become home to people from
more than a dozen European nations and innumerable African tribes, as well
as to the surviving Native Americans. If the conventional wisdom was correct
that state-enforced religious conformity was a prerequisite for social harmony
and the regulation of morality, the settlements clustered along the Atlantic coast
should have been an absolute disaster. That these divergent groups could live
together under English rule in relative harmony seemed a near miracle. The
idea that they would ever successfully rule themselves without a bloodbath
would have been judged preposterous. Yet religious equality, in itself a radical
idea, would ultimately be the only ground upon which these various groups
could come together to create a single nation.

V.1. Numerous editions of the
History of the Holy Jesus, a
book intended for children,
were published in New England
beginning in ca. 1745. The
woodcuts in this edition are
crude, but their message is
representative of the concern
for piety felt by many people at
mid-century.

The careful MOTHER instructing her CHILDREN.

ABRAHAM offering up his Son ISAAC.

The CHILD's *Body* of DIVINITY.

A DAM by's Fall bro't Death on all.

B Y his foul Sin we've ruin'd been.

C HRIST Jesus come to ranfom fome.

D ARE any fay this an't the Way.

CHAPTER V   # Conflicting Trends in Eighteenth-Century Colonial Religion

Much of the variation in colonial religion was imported. Settlers brought their faith with them from their native countries. But other variations developed in the New World after these settlers had arrived. Two different religious trends in particular emerged in the eighteenth century that threatened to divide the colonists into opposing camps. First, religious revivals swept through the colonies beginning in the late 1730s, converting many to a highly emotional, deeply personal Christianity. At the same time, although over a longer period, other colonists moved toward a less emotional, more rational approach to religiosity. These two groups, the evangelical and the liberal, seemed destined to oppose one another. Yet despite real contention, they did ultimately find some common ground for concerted action, coming together to a remarkable extent in the American Revolution.

Revivalism and Evangelical Religion

Christians often enjoy a profoundly moving experience of their faith. The act of conversion usually involves a heightened sense of one's sinfulness, followed by the realization that Christ will forgive these sins if the sinner has faith in Him. Many colonial churches emphasized conversion, an experience that was usually private and individual, as a necessary stage in the development of a true believer. The religious revivals of the eighteenth century, however, transformed this individual conversion into a group experience in which large numbers of people converted at the same time and apparently in response to the same stimulus. It is interesting to note that all of Western Europe was undergoing a comparable quickening of religious piety during this time. Although historians have long debated their cause, such large-scale conversions were frequently sparked by some particularly inspiring preacher. These revivals might occur within already existing congregations, where they would stimulate a renewed concern with spiritual matters, or among previously unchurched people attending church for the first time.

The first major revival of the eighteenth century has been called the "Great Awakening," for it seemed to some observers to rouse people out of a growing spiritual stupor. The first indications of a revival could be seen in a few congregations in New England, where some ministers impressed upon their flocks the importance of faith, or "saving grace," in the life of a true Christian. The great theologian Jonathan Edwards (figure V.4.) reported such an outpouring of the spirit in his Northampton, Massachusetts, congregation in 1734–35.

The real explosion in religious fervor began in 1739, when George Whitefield made the first in a series of preaching tours through the American colonies (figure V.1.). "The Grand Itinerant," as Whitefield was called, was an Anglican

A POEM,

On the joyful News of the Rev. Mr. *Whitefield*'s Visit to *Boston*.

Dedicated to all the true Friends of such " an exemplary Christian, fine Gentleman and accomplish'd Orator, who has discover'd in some late Sermons such a deep Insight into human Nature, which abounded with fine Characters, curiously pourtray'd, and his great Skill in moral Penciling, which with his Manner of Life, he's justly gain'd this Character.

IS blessed *Whitefield* come again ?
   Our Hearts does now rejoyce,
We pray good People all attend
   And hear his lovely Voice.
2
For fourteen Years he has been try'd
   By Enemies and Friends ;
And now upon this new Return
   The heavenly Sound it rings.
3
Behold the charming, Smiling Man,
   Something of Heaven appears ;
His Countenance so pleasant is,
   And Voice that charms our Ears.
4
See how Opposers hang their Heads,
   And joyful Saints arise,
A Man is come who fears them not,
   In whom's no Cowardize.
5
He certainly is a good Man,
   Which Envy can't deny,
For he has done those Things which none
   Has in our Memory.
6
The Gospel pure, comes from his Lips,
   The Law has its due Place,
Men are convinc'd of Sin and Guilt,
   Who afterwards finds Peace.
7
Not that we would insinuate,
   Or Reflections throw
On those brave Men, who've done their best,
   As God does only know.
8
But should we now offend the World,
   We must and will declare
He is the Man of whom there's none,
   For us we can compare.
9
He calculated so well is
   By the great God above,
To reach the Hearts of Sinners here,
   Which fills our Souls with Love.
10
With honest Freedom he's declar'd,
   The *Inward Call* he's got ;
And if Experience won't convince,
   Reason we're sure will not.
11
But not for to dispute the Fact,
   Let's all unite as one,
And each examine for himself,
   As God is Judge alone.
12
You'll hear by and by the heavenly Sound
   Flow from his charming Tongue,
Rebellious Men be seiz'd with Fear,
   And with Conviction stung ;
13
While Saints and all the heavenly Train
   With Rapture and Surprize,
Exulting are in Joys Above,
   To see us gain the Prize.
14
Should Churches now be shut,
   The Field's wide open stand,
Where ev'ry one with Freedom may
   Hear the great God's Commands.
15
Transported with the Thoughts of this
   It animates our Love,

To follow him as he does Christ,
   Who reigns with God above.
16
Let Men unite, and Priests combine,
   Freedom we will maintain,
Our Consciences we must discharge
   Religion for to gain.
17
The Gentleman and Christ'an too
   United are we see,
The Orator and Reasoner,
   How natural and free?
18
If any will, like him, set out,
   Be honest in their Aims,
Convince the World, as he has done,
   Who seeks not his own Gain,
19
They then shall have like Praise which he
   In Justice claims from us:
But don't pretend, unless you can,
   Like him, be very just.
20
You know the Credit he has giv'n
   Of all he has receiv'd ;
Let any one judge as he will,
   The Poor by him's reliev'd.
21
He hoards not up, as many do,
   But lib'rally bestows,
The Charity which he receives,
   His Enemies well knows.
22
Then why should Honesty in him
   Whose Vertues shine so bright,
Be clouded by some wicked Men,
   Whose Deeds are dark as Night.
23
But as a Tree which good Fruit bears,
   Is often beat and bruis'd,
So this dear Friend, by many has
   Most cruelly been us'd.
24
And now our dearest Brethren come,
   If you with us agree,
And let us join our Hearts and Hands,
   Whitefield's to preach to Day.
25
Let's for a while our worldly Thoughts
   And anxious Cares resign,
The Man is come of whom we think,
   Something in him's divine.
26
He still goes on, as you may see,
   His Master's Cause maintains,
And in the end, no Doubt he will
   Ascend the heavenly Plains,
27
Where Envy, Tattling and all Lies
   Forever's at an End,
And Peace and Love enjoy'd by those,
   Who've made their God their Friend.
28
Ye Widows all pray now attend,
   And little Maidens too,
Ye pretty Boys and little Girls,
   For *Whitefield* calls to you.
29
The *Negroes* too he'll not forget,
   But tells them all to come ;
Invites the *Black* as well as *White*,
   And says for them there's Room.

BOSTON, Printed Oct. 1754.

V.2. This broadside from 1754, published on the occasion of George Whitefield's second major tour of the colonies, defended the great preacher against various attacks leveled against him in the preceding fifteen years.

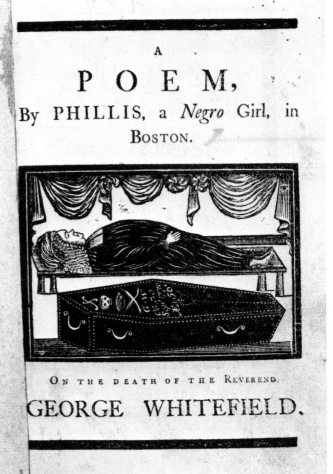

A POEM, By PHILLIS, a *Negro* Girl, in BOSTON.

ON THE DEATH OF THE REVEREND GEORGE WHITEFIELD.

V.3. The poet Phillis Wheatley (see figure IV.12.) was one of many mourners of Whitefield upon his death in 1770. This elegy was published in Boston in that year.

minister whose tours ostensibly were undertaken for the purpose of raising money for an orphanage in Georgia. His preaching proved so stirring that huge crowds came out to hear him, and many people were converted. He preached in churches, town halls, and open fields all over the colonies to people of many different faiths.

Whitefield was soon succeeded by other preachers, most notably the Presbyterian Gilbert Tennent and the Congregationalist James Davenport. The tours of these major itinerants were supplemented on the local level by many gifted men who preached to their friends, neighbors, and congregations. To the pious, the time seemed ripe for a general upsurge in religiosity.

72
George Whitefield (1714–1770).
A Continuation of the Reverend Mr. Whitefield's Journal.
(London, 1740)

The Reverend George Whitefield was a minister in the Anglican Church, and was involved in a reform movement within the Church that would eventually lead to the establishment of Methodism as a separate denomination. He came to America to found an orphanage in the newly settled colony of Georgia, and in 1739 and 1740 made preaching tours up and down the Atlantic seaboard to raise money for this charitable endeavor. His charismatic preaching had an effect felt far beyond the Georgia orphanage, however, for the sporadic revivals that had occurred in isolated communities in the preceding years grew and spread through Whitefield's efforts (figure V.2. and 3.).

73
Jonathan Edwards (1703–1758).
A Treatise Concerning Religious Affections.
(Boston, 1746)

At the death of his grandfather Solomon Stoddard, Jonathan Edwards took charge of the congregation in Northampton, Massachusetts. Under his ministry, the community experienced a spiritual revival which was described by Edwards in a pamphlet published in 1737. When this revival and others like it were attacked by the Boston minister Charles Chauncy as being irrational, Edwards responded with this *Treatise Concerning Religious Affections*, an attempt to explicate the conversion experience and to describe the signs of true piety. In this work Edwards revealed a sophisticated understanding of the workings of the human psyche, grounding religious experience in emotion or affection more than in intellect. In this and other works he made a major contribution to theology, and his thought had a profound impact on subsequent generations of American intellectuals. One of the greatest defenders of religious revivalism, Edwards belied the stereotype of the ill-educated pietistic preacher (figure V.4.).

Some people opposed the religious enthusiasm of the Great Awakening (figure V.2.). They claimed that the converts did not understand the Christian faith very well, and were simply overcome with emotion. Anti-revivalists were labeled "Old Lights" because they preferred the traditional, more sedate religious atmosphere to which they were accustomed. Old Light ministers sometimes refused to relinquish their pulpits to visiting evangelists, and even preached against the revivals. When the increasingly unstable itinerant James Davenport led a group of converts in burning books and fine clothes in a symbolic renunciation of the learning and wealth of this world, Old Lights asserted that Davenport's excesses were the natural result of the unbridled enthusiasm of the Awakeners. Many pro-revivalists dismissed Davenport as a fanatic but held to their views on the general benefits of the Awakening. Congregations frequently split over this issue, with one faction breaking away to form their own church. In this way many New England towns came to maintain two Congregational churches, one Old Light and one New.

In the years after this initial outpouring of religious fervor, Presbyterian and, later, Baptist ministers launched intensive efforts to spread their faiths throughout the southern colonies. These efforts brought many conversions, particularly among slaves and settlers in the back country. The Presbyterian minister Samuel Davies, in his struggle to win the right to preach unmolested by the authorities, challenged the Church of England's privileged position in Virginia. The supremacy of the Anglican church in the south was severely shaken during the quarter of a century leading up to the American Revolution.

The main beneficiaries of the increase in evangelical religious sentiments in the southern colonies were the Baptist churches. The few Baptist churches that were in existence before 1740 were divided over doctrinal issues such as whether salvation was possible for all, or only for the elect. It was only after the Great Awakening that the Baptist faith became one of the preeminent denominations in the North American colonies. The intense conversion experience associated with the revivals convinced many people to undergo adult baptism to seal their new relationship with God. Between 1740 and 1770 Baptist churches in the three southern New England colonies increased from twenty-five to seventy-eight. After 1750 churches in the northern and middle colonies sponsored the missionary efforts in the south that would result in the phenomenal growth in Baptist churches there by the end of the century.

The Great Awakening and the periodic revivals that followed it, especially in the southern colonies, initiated a tradition of revivalism that has continued to shape American culture. Two important effects of the eighteenth-century religious revivals were the undermining of the efforts of certain colonies to maintain an established church, and the increase of religious fragmentation throughout the colonies.

V.4. Jonathan Edwards, from the frontispiece of *The Millennium* (Elizabethtown, New Jersey, 1794), a compilation of three essays on the subject, edited by David Austin. One of the essays was by Edwards.

74
Jonathan Edwards.
Sinners in the Hands of an Angry God.
(Boston, 1745)

Jonathan Edwards was not only a great theologian; he was also capable of preaching profoundly moving, often deeply disturbing, sermons. This sermon, originally delivered to the congregation in the neighboring town of Enfield, Connecticut, in 1741, revealed Edwards's gift for creating suspense through the use of gripping imagery. Impressing people with a sense of their sinfulness, *Sinners in the Hands of an Angry God* was carefully orchestrated to bring a congregation to repent and convert. Although this work was certainly not Edward's greatest intellectual endeavor, it has rightly been recognized as a great literary achievement, one still capable of gripping its reader today.

75
James Davenport (1716–1757).
Confession and Retractions.
(Boston, 1744)

Like Edwards, James Davenport was the product of an old New England family and a graduate of Yale. He had been minister of a church in Southold, Long Island, for only a few years when the Great Awakening began. In 1741 he took up the life of an itinerant minister, hoping to follow in the path of the great George Whitefield. Davenport's sermons usually contained denunciations of local unconverted ministers. More than any other well-known New Light preacher, Davenport would single out ministers he found to be lacking in godliness and encourage their congregations to oust these men in order to save their own souls. After a bookburning he led brought almost universal condemnation and threatened to bring the Awakening into disrepute, Davenport was persuaded to publish this *Confession and Retractions*. If Edwards offered the best example of a man who combined a great intellect with the emotion associated with religious revival, Davenport represented his antithesis, a man unable or unwilling to combine the two effectively.

Liberal Religion

While the eighteenth century was a time of widespread religious revival in the colonies, it was also a period of intense intellectual change associated with a movement known as the Enlightenment. The Enlightenment was a complex movement, with far-reaching effects, that developed out of the philosophical and scientific inquiry of the preceding two centuries. European intellectuals had been jolted by the work of such men as Sir Isaac Newton into rethinking many traditional ideas and into coming to view the natural world as ordered and reasonable. Enlightenment thinkers were fortified with the conviction that the universe and man's place in it could be understood rationally, and they set out to apply the new scientific methods to every aspect of life. The movement generated high hopes for the potential for progress, fostering the belief that traditional attitudes and institutions hampered the discovery of the natural order.

These ideas encouraged a reexamination of traditional Christianity, for advocates of the Enlightenment preferred religious beliefs that seemed rooted in reason over those that had to be accepted on faith. With such great emphasis on the intellect and on the human potential, this rational approach to religion rejected the view that man was depraved, and it presented God as a benevolent but increasingly impersonal diety. Religion, it was believed, ought to be primarily a matter of moral observance, not of ritual or of intricate theology. The proponents of rational religion never formed a single party, but applied these ideas in a variety of ways. Historians sometimes use the term "liberals" when referring to the amorphous group that embraced these views.

One early example of the impact of this liberal, or rational, approach to Christianity in the colonies occurred in 1699 when a group of merchants and other substantial citizens in Boston founded a new church, the Brattle Street Church. Although these founders did not abandon the idea that God had predestined a few individuals for salvation, they did institute a number of reforms that were liberal by Puritan New England standards. This new church placed much less emphasis on the "elect," allowing any reputable person to participate in the Lord's Supper or to vote on church business. In the Brattle Street Church *Manifesto*, the communicants cited the "laws of nature" as well as the Scriptures to justify their innovations. Later generations of rationalists would rely on these "laws" in their search for a reasoned understanding of the universe and man's place in it.

During the eighteenth century the liberal religion that the Brattle Street Church first faintly sanctioned took on a more general significance. For most of the colonial period, a religious liberal did not belong to any particular church, embracing instead a liberal stance while remaining within one of the existing denominations. A few congregations, particularly those in urban areas, moved gradually and almost imperceptibly toward rationalism. Usually, colonists remained within the general Christian mainstream while participating in the secularizing trend that the Enlightenment encouraged.

Liberal beliefs varied in degree. Sometimes liberals rejected the doctrine of predestination, believing that all of humanity was capable of being saved. English advocates of universal redemption established a sect called Universalists, and the first American Universalist church was founded in Gloucester, Massachusetts, in 1779. Other liberals questioned the idea of the Trinity. Unitarianism, which has been called the quintessential expression of liberalism in early-American religion, earned its name because of its adherents' disbelief in the concept of God as three distinct persons. The most extreme position a rationalist might take was atheism, the utter rejection of the existence of God.

Universalism, Unitarianism, and atheism had to wait for the post-Revolutionary years to be freely espoused, and even then atheists were always viewed with suspicion or even hostility. Before that time, the component ideas of all these views and others were bandied about without any formal groups coalescing around them.

Probably the most pervasive rational religious position adopted in colonial society was deism. Before the American Revolution, deism was not a religion in any organized sense, but a philosophical movement that touched many people's religious beliefs. As a result, deism was simply a constellation of beliefs rather than a specific creed, and varied from one individual to another.

Most deists held that God created the universe so that it functioned according to natural laws that were comprehensible to the human mind. Thus, they shunned the idea that God expressed his pleasure or displeasure with humanity through divine providence, which so many Christians had watched for during the seventeenth century. Instead, deists thought God had created a mechanical universe in which nothing happened arbitrarily. A few went so far as to reject all revealed religion, arguing that only that which could be grasped through reason could be considered true. Thomas Jefferson, for instance, offered a typical example of such reasoning when he concluded that Jesus Christ was primarily a great moral teacher, rather than a divine savior. Deists were often accused by their detractors of advocating atheism, but deists did believe in God; their conception of God was simply very different from that of traditional Christianity.

Liberal religion was a broad category, encompassing some New England Old Lights like Charles Chauncy, who advocated a rational approach within the framework of traditional religion, and radical deists, who rejected most traditional Christian beliefs. One scholar has noted that both the revivals and the Enlightenment constituted a rejection, albeit in opposite directions, of the complicated theological disputes and intense doctrinal differences that the Protestant Reformation had unleashed. On the eve of the Revolution those who approached religion with their intellects appeared destined to remain at odds with those who emphasized the emotional element in their faith.

76
John Locke (1632–1704).
A Letter Concerning Toleration.
(Boston, 1743)

Sometimes called "America's philosopher" because of the impact of his ideas on eighteenth-century American intellectuals, Locke was a pivotal figure in the development of Enlightenment thought. For instance, his *Essay Concerning Human Understanding* (1690) influenced the theologian Jonathan Edwards, while his *Two Treatises of Government* (1690) informed the Revolutionary documents composed by Thomas Jefferson. Locke embraced the liberal view that the primary goal of religion was "the regulating of Mens Lives according to the Rules of Vertue and Piety." Because persecution was by definition unchristian, Locke advocated the toleration of all beliefs as long as they did not pose an extreme threat to civil peace. Locke took advantage of the new freedoms enjoyed in England after the Glorious Revolution of 1689 to publish his works for the

first time. *A Letter Concerning Toleration* was issued in that year. In 1743, responding to the intolerant position adopted by the Yale president and governors during the Great Awakening, some members of the senior class contributed toward the publication of a reprint of Locke's *Letter.* The president of Yale, Thomas Clap, supposedly threatened to withhold degrees from any students who refused to make a public confession of their part in the project. Despite President Clap's objections, this edition went to press in Boston.

77

Charles Chauncy (1705–1787).
Enthusiasm Described and Caution'd Against.
(Boston, 1742)

Charles Chauncy, for many years the minister of Boston's First Church, became increasingly involved throughout his lifetime in the rational religious movement. He came out against the Great Awakening in sermons and in print, prompting Jonathan Edwards to respond by publishing his pro-revival works. *Enthusiasm Described and Caution'd Against* traced the New Lights back to all the mystical "heresies" that challenged the New England Way over the years. Chauncy saw a natural progression from Anne Hutchinson and the antinomians through the Quakers down to the revivalists of his own day. Chauncy presented his viewpoint in numerous important pamphlets and, near the end of his life, published anonymously a defense of the doctrine of universal redemption.

78

Ethan Allen (1738–1789).
Reason the Only Oracle of Man.
(Bennington, Vermont, 1784)

This famous pamphlet by Ethan Allen was the first deist work published in the United States. Allen's views were shared by many other Revolutionary leaders, including Thomas Jefferson, Benjamin Franklin, and John Adams. Unlike these contemporaries, Allen was primarily a war hero and local politician, and was not as adept with his pen. This, his only publication, indicated how widespread deist ideas were becoming. Allen had developed his position fairly independently. He confided in the preface to this work that although his acquaintances tell him he is a deist, he has never read any deist works. This edition, the first, is very rare, because a fire at the printer's shop destroyed most copies. Legend has it that the printer intentionally burned still more of the first-edition copies because of what he considered to be their atheistic content.

79

Thomas Paine (1737–1809).
The Age of Reason.
(Boston, 1794)

The greatest deist work of any age was Thomas Paine's *The Age of Reason*. Although Paine was an Englishman and this work was first published in France, both the man and the tract came to have a special place in American history. Paine moved to Philadelphia from England in 1774 and immediately became involved in the patriot cause. *Common Sense*, published in 1776, was unquestionably the single most important pamphlet of the Revolutionary era. In simple language that everyone could understand, Paine advocated revolution and the establishment of a republic. After Paine returned to Europe in 1787, he became involved in the French Revolution, and published a number of other radical works. *The Age of Reason* created a huge controversy in the United States because many Americans were unwilling to accept Paine's assertion that a revolution in government ought to be accompanied by one in religion. Paine was falsely accused of atheism, an epithet that would later be used against his political ally, Jefferson, during the year before the latter's election to the presidency in 1800 (figure V.5.).

V.5. This portrait of Thomas Paine is from the London 1792 edition of *The Rights of Man*.

SOME POETICAL THOUGHTS
On the DIFFICULTIES our FORE-FATHERS
endured in planting Religious and civil LIBERTY,
In this Weſtern WORLD.

With a few HINTS on the preſent STATE of AFFAIRS.

V.6. In 1776 thoughts of liberty were uppermost, as was evidenced by this broadside, published in New Haven in that year.

Coming Together in Revolution

Despite the differences that divided them, the evangelicals and the rationalists were able to put aside these differences to find common cause in the American Revolution. Religious liberals participated in the Revolution for some very obvious reasons. Believing that man ought to apply empirical scientific methods to every facet of life in order to discover the natural laws that governed it, rationalists adopted a reasoned, scientific approach to government as well as to religion. Many of the most famous Revolutionary leaders were rationalists in both realms. These attitudes created an important bond between them and a foundation upon which to build.

Evangelicals often embraced the Revolutionary cause, though their reasons for doing so were related to their religious position in more subtle ways. The revivals fostered a sense that the colonies were special in the eyes of God and destined for great things. The New England Puritans had considered themselves chosen by God to erect a Biblical commonwealth in the wilderness. This sense of themselves as a chosen people was revived, and it spread to other areas. The Revolution seemed to present a special opportunity to overthrow tyranny and to create a more virtuous state, free of Old World corruptions (figure V.6.).

Revolutionary rhetoric often cast the struggle in religious terms, with the evil British imperial power trying to crush the godly colonists. Since proponents of revival placed greater emphasis on a person's godliness than on education or social status, this served to encourage democratic attitudes—attitudes that would have profound political consequences. Thus were the evangelicals prepared for revolution.

80
Jonathan Mayhew (1720–1766).
The Snare Broken.
(Boston, 1766)

Jonathan Mayhew was a liberal minister and an ardent patriot. Before his untimely death in 1766, Mayhew opposed the British policies that would eventually lead to the American Revolution. When Parliament passed a law requiring all documents to bear a tax stamp as part of Britain's effort to raise revenue from the colonies, the Americans protested until the Act was repealed. Mayhew preached *The Snare Broken* upon the repeal of the Stamp Act. The sermon's title reflected his perception of the Act as some sort of trap set for the colonists. His advice about how to deal with any further snares was heeded by his audience, although Mayhew would not live to see it.

Although the disagreements between liberals and evangelicals represented a potentially divisive force, the spread throughout the colonies of Enlightenment thought and Christian pietism also united people. As we have seen, the colonists had traditionally been divided along ethnic and denominational lines, as well as those of class and color. The religious revivals and the spread of rationalism drew people together, albeit into two separate camps. An Anglican with deist tendencies living in Virginia in 1760 had a great deal more in common with a liberal New England Congregationalist than with either of their counterparts of a century before. Similarly, a German Lutheran Pietist enjoyed sermons by the Anglican revivalist preacher George Whitefield, even when language differences might have created a barrier. In one reported case, a German-speaking woman derived great spiritual comfort from his preaching although she understood no English at all. When colonists came together to deal with the problems created by British imperial policies, many of them found they shared common experiences that fostered similar attitudes about their situation. These two religious trends, conflicting though they were, helped to create a common culture that united all colonists.

V.7. An example of the fusion of certain religious and political expectations among American patriots.

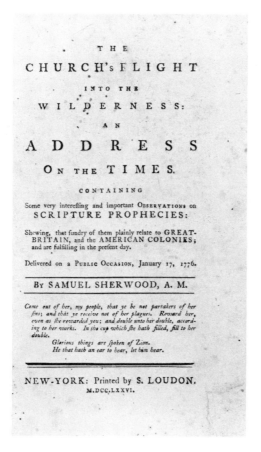

81
Samuel Sherwood (1730–1783).
The Church's Flight into the Wilderness.
(New York, 1776)

For centuries Christians have been awaiting the apocalyptic events prophesied in the Book of Revelation, and no more so than during times of historic upheaval. The American Revolution was thus understood by many in terms of these scriptural prophecies. In this sermon, Connecticut Congregationalist minister Samuel Sherwood interpreted the imperial struggle in this apocalyptic context. Such religious rhetoric fortified patriots in their cause, making it easier to take the revolutionary step of overthrowing British rule in favor of their own political independence (figure V.7.).

82
Amos Adams (1728–1775).
Religious Liberty an Invaluable Blessing.
(Boston, 1768)

The Revolutionary struggle made many people more aware of individual rights in every sphere. While political freedoms were being debated, the injustice of American slavery and the importance of religious liberty were widely discussed for the first time. Regardless of their religious affiliations, many Americans were coming to agree with Congregationalist Amos Adams about *Religious Liberty an Invaluable Blessing.*

Quebec Bill

The Mitre · Minuet.

C Revere sc.

VI.1. This cartoon, number 15 in a series, from the *Royal American Magazine,* volume I, number 10 (Boston, 1774), illustrates the fear among the colonists, especially in New England, that the Church of England was conspiring with political powers in Britain to suppress American liberties. Paul Revere engraved this copy from a plate that originally appeared in the *London Magazine.*

CHAPTER VI

Liberty of Conscience Endorsed

Today we almost take for granted that the residents of the thirteen British colonies were able to unite, first in rebellion against the English crown and then once again in forming a new nation. To many observers at the time, however, the people living in those colonies seemed too diverse to be able to reach agreement on creating a new government. In fact, large numbers of people—Loyalists—opposed the initial revolt against the King, and some fled the country after the patriots succeeded. Another substantial group were simply unconcerned with the larger political struggle, at least until it touched their own lives.

The American Revolution was a complex event, understood in many contradictory ways by the participants as well as by later historians. Yet it is apparent that religion played a major role in shaping the Revolutionary years and, as we have seen, many people understood the Revolution as a spiritual struggle. Some thought the 1770s must be ushering in the apocalypse as foretold in *Revelations*. Particularly in New England, some colonists were distressed by the fact that Great Britain granted French Catholics in Canada freedom of worship in the Quebec Act of 1774, and by renewed discussion of the Church of England's plan to send an Anglican bishop to the American colonies (figure VI.1.). Others hesitated to support the patriots because they feared a patriot victory would result in persecution of minority religious groups. This concern was shared by many non-English or non-Protestant colonists who thought that the English Protestant patriot leaders might use their new power to persecute others. Even English Protestant minority denominations, such as the Baptists, worried that New England Congregationalists or Virginia Anglicans might try to reassert their favored position once the laws of Great Britian no longer held them in check. Because large segments of the population were threatened by the religious consequences of a patriot victory, the assurance by the revolutionaries that they supported the principle of liberty of conscience undermined one source of opposition to the patriot cause.

83
John Adams (1735–1826).
An Essay on Canon and Feudal Law.
(Philadelphia, 1783)

An Essay on Canon and Feudal Law was originally written in four installments that appeared anonymously in the *Boston Gazette* in 1765. Adams was among those who joined in the Revolutionary struggle to protect liberties long enjoyed in the colonies. Here he attributed those freedoms to the absence of repressive European legal systems and the comparatively high level of literacy in North America. Distressed by the recently repealed Stamp Act, by the Quebec Act (see figure VI.1.), and by rumors that an Anglican bishop was to be installed in the colonies, Adams suggested that a plot was afoot to rob America of her traditional liberties. Always faithful to his original goal of protecting the colonial system he so revered, Adams in later years opposed attempts to transform the American social and political order. For example, he resisted the movement to disestablish religion in Massachusetts. Adams believed that the limited toleration granted to dissenters through the certification system was adequate.

Isaac Backus (1724–1806).
A History of New England with Particular Reference to the Denomination of Christians called Baptists. 3 vols. (Boston, 1777, 1784, 1796)

The great Baptist minister Isaac Backus had experienced conversion during the Great Awakening in his native Norwich, Connecticut. He soon felt called to preach and took up the life of an itinerant, eventually settling down as the pastor of a congregation in Middleborough, Connecticut. Later he led part of his flock into the Baptist fold after he had come to accept that denomination as the true religion. Backus wrote this history during the Revolutionary years. Though he hoped for the day when all America would embrace the Baptist faith, Backus advocated legal religious equality as a way to protect those he considered true believers until such a day came. Backus's history chronicled the struggle of one minority religious group to secure that equality, a struggle that ultimately benefited all religious minorities.

---

32   IN THE TENTH YEAR OF THE COMMONWEALTH.

1786.

against the Surveyor, or other delinquent, and if no reasonable excuse be made for such default, may give judgment for the penalty and costs, not exceeding twenty-five shillings, or such offenders may be presented by the Grand Juries; in all which cases of conviction, on view of a Justice, or presentment, or on private informations to Justices, where there shall be no evidence to convict the offender but the informer's own oath, the whole penalties shall be to the use of the County, towards lessening the levy thereof, and shall be annually collected and accounted for by the Sheriff, in the same manner as County levies; and to enable the Sheriff to make such collection, every Justice, immediately on conviction of any offender, where the penalty is to be to the County, shall certify the same to the Clerk of his County Court, who shall yearly, before the first day of March, deliver to the Sheriff a list of all the offenders so certified, and of all others convicted in Court, within one year preceding, of any offence against this Act.

To be prosecuted for within six months.

XII. PROVIDED, That prosecutions for any offence herein mentioned, shall be commenced within six months after the offence committed, and not after.

Commencement of this act.

XIII. THIS Act shall commence and be in force from and after the first day of January, one thousand seven hundred and eighty-seven.

C H A P.   XX.

An Act for establishing Religious Freedom.

[Passed the 16th of December, 1785.]

Preamble.

I. WHEREAS Almighty God hath created the mind free; that all attempts to influence it by temporal punishments or burthens, or by civil incapacitations, tend only to beget habits of hypocrisy and meanness, and are a departure from the plan of the Holy Author of our religion, who being Lord both of body and mind, yet chose not to propagate it by coercions on either, as was in his Almighty power to do; that the impious presumption of Legislators and Rulers, civil as well as ecclesiastical, who being themselves but fallible and uninspired men, have assumed dominion over the faith of others, setting up their own opinions and modes of thinking as the only true and infallible, and as such endeavouring to impose them on others, hath established and maintained false religions over the greatest part of the world, and through all time; that to compel a man to furnish contributions of money for the propagation of opinions which he disbelieves, is sinful and tyrannical; that even the forcing him to support this or that teacher of his own religious persuasion, is depriving him of the comfortable liberty of giving his contributions to the particular pastor, whose morals he would make his pattern, and whose powers he feels most persuasive to righteousness, and is withdrawing from the ministry those temporary rewards, which proceeding from an approbation of their personal conduct, are an additional incitement to earnest and unremitting labours for the instruction of mankind; that our civil rights have no dependence on our religious opinions, any more than our opinions in physics or geometry; that therefore the proscribing any Citizen as unworthy the public confidence, by laying upon him an incapacity of being called to offices of trust and emolument, unless he professs, or renounce this or that religious opinion, is depriving him injuriously, of those privileges and advantages, to which, in common with his fellow-citizens, he has a natural right; that it tends only to corrupt the principles of that religion it is meant to encourage, by bribing with a monopoly of worldly honours and emoluments, those who will externally profess and conform to it; that though indeed these are criminal who do not withstand such temptation, yet neither are those innocent who lay the bait in their way; that to suffer the civil Magistrate to intrude his powers into the field of opinion, and to restrain the profession or propagation of principles on supposition of their ill tendency, is a dangerous fallacy, which at once destroys all religious liberty, because he being of course judge of that tendency, will make his opinions the rule of judgment, and approve or condemn the sentiments of others only as they shall square with or differ from his own; that it is time enough for the rightful purposes of civil government, for its officers to interfere when principles break out into overt acts against peace and good order; and finally, that truth is great and will prevail if left to herself; that she is the proper and sufficient antagonist to error, and has nothing to fear from the conflict, unless by human in-

---

IN THE ELEVENTH YEAR OF THE COMMONWEALTH.   33

1786.

terposition disarmed of her natural weapons, free argument and debate, errors ceasing to be dangerous when it is permitted freely to contradict them:

No man compelled to frequent or support any religious worship. All men free to profess, and by argument to maintain their religious opinions.

II. BE it enacted by the General Assembly, That no man shall be compelled to frequent or support any religious worship, place, or Ministry whatsoever, nor shall be enforced, restrained, molested, or burthened in his body or goods, nor shall otherwise suffer on account of his religious opinions or belief; but that all men shall be free to profess, and by argument to maintain, their opinions in matters of religion, and that the same shall in no wise diminish, enlarge, or affect their civil capacities.

Declaration that the rights by this Act asserted, are of the natural rights of mankind.

III. AND though we well know that this Assembly elected by the people for the ordinary purposes of legislation only, have no power to restrain the Acts of succeeding Assemblies, constituted with powers equal to our own, and that therefore to declare this Act to be irrevocable, would be of no effect in law; yet we are free to declare, and do declare, that the rights hereby asserted, are of the natural rights of mankind, and that if any Act shall be hereafter passed to repeal the present, or to narrow its operation, such Act will be an infringement of natural right.

General Assembly, begun and held at the Public Buildings, in the City of Richmond, on Monday, the 16th Day of October, in the Year of our Lord, 1786.

C H A P.   XXI.

An Act forbidding and punishing Affrays.

[Passed the 27th of November, 1786.]

Punishment of persons going armed before Courts of Justice, or the other Ministers of Justice, or in fairs or markets in terror of the Country.

BE it enacted by the General Assembly, That no man, great nor small, of what condition soever he be, except the Ministers of Justice in executing the precepts of the Courts of Justice, or in executing of their office, and such as be in their company assisting them, be so hardy to come before the Justices of any Court, or other of their Ministers of Justice, doing their office, with force and arms, on pain, to forfeit their armour to the Commonwealth, and their bodies to prison, at the pleasure of a Court; nor go nor ride armed by night nor by day, in fairs or markets, or in other places, in terror of the Country, upon pain of being arrested and committed to prison by any Justice on his own view, or proof by others, there to abide for so long a time as a Jury, to be sworn for that purpose by the said Justice, shall direct, and in like manner to forfeit his armour to the Commonwealth; but no person shall be imprisoned for such offence by a longer space of time than one month.

C H A P.   XXII.

An Act against Conspirators.

[Passed the 27th of November, 1786.]

Who shall be deemed conspirators.

BE it declared and enacted by the General Assembly, That Conspirators be they that do confederate and bind themselves by oath, covenant, or other alliance, that every of them shall aid and bear the other falsely and maliciously, to move or cause to be moved any indictment or information against another on the part of the Commonwealth, and those who are convicted thereof at the suit of the Commonwealth, shall be punished by imprisonment and amercement, at the discretion of a Jury.

I

VI.3. This printing of Jefferson's "Act for Establishing Freedom of Religion," which was passed by the Virginia legislature in 1786, appeared in an official publication of the state, *A Collection of all such Acts of the General Assembly of Virginia, of a Public and Permanent Nature, as are Now in Force* (Richmond, 1794).

VI.2. This engraving of Jefferson appeared as the frontispiece of the eighth edition of his *Notes on the State of Virginia* (Boston, 1801).

Aside from any considerations of the political benefits of such a stance, the right to liberty of conscience was an inherent part of American Revolutionary ideology. The government that the patriots sought to erect was theoretically based on the voluntary association of individuals, all of whom enjoyed the freedom to choose. Liberty of conscience was one of the freedoms such an experiment in republican government required. Many of the leading patriots in the cause against England were also important advocates in the fight for liberty of conscience. These men were consciously going against the wisdom of the ages in erecting a new form of government and in instituting a new policy toward religion.

Thomas Jefferson (figure VI.2.) was in some ways the preeminent revolutionary. As a young lawyer he stood in the back of the Virginia legislature, mesmerized by the stirring words of Patrick Henry during the early years of the conflict over British policy. He was himself elected to the House of Burgesses in 1769, and participated in the developing patriot faction. In 1776, as a delegate to the revolutionary Continental Congress, Jefferson was asked to compose the Declaration of Independence; he was, at the time, only thirty-three years old.

Soon after, Jefferson turned his attention to reforming Virginia's colonial laws for the use of that newly founded state. In 1777 he drafted the "Act for Establishing Freedom of Religion," which would eventually assure religious liberty in Virginia and would set the tone for other Revolutionary documents on this question (figure VI.3.). After a stint as governor of Virginia, Jefferson was chosen to serve as ambassador to France, the new nation's most important ally. While in France, Jefferson received news of the passage of his "Act for Establishing Freedom of Religion" (1786) and of the ratification of the U.S. Constitution (1787). In his correspondence to his many patriot friends in the United States, Jefferson urged the passage of a bill of rights to safeguard the freedoms for which they had all fought. He returned in time to witness the passage of the Bill of Rights by the First Congress in 1790. The first freedom the Bill protected was that of religion, stating "the Congress shall make no laws respecting an establishment of religion or prohibiting the free exercise thereof."

85
A Collection of all such Acts of the General Assembly of Virginia, of a Public and Permanent Nature, as are Now in Force.
(Richmond, 1794)

This collection included the "Act for Establishing Freedom of Religion in Virginia," the first major move toward adopting liberty of conscience during the Revolutionary era. Composed by Jefferson, the Act was passed only after a struggle in the Virginia legislature (figure VI.3.).

86
Thomas Jefferson (1742–1826)
Notes on the State of Virginia.
([Paris, 1785])

Written in 1781 in answer to a set of questions sent by a French official to every state, Jefferson's *Notes* presented a thorough account of Virginia's history and current situation. Among other things, Jefferson treated the Anglican establishment in the colony and advocated complete religious equality as a substitute for it. The *Notes* were composed after he had written his bill proposing religious freedom, but before that act had been passed. Originally privately printed in 1785 for distribution among his friends, Jefferson's *Notes* were published the following year, without the author's permission, in French. Because the first French edition was poorly done, Jefferson was persuaded to prepare an authorized edition for publication. *Notes on the State of Virginia* subsequently went through numerous editions.

(12)

themfelves, nor by an authority derived from them, and are flaves.

Becaufe, it is proper to take alarm at the firft experiment on our liberties. We hold this prudent jealoufy to be the firft duty of citizens, and one of the nobleft characteriftics of the late revolution. The freemen of America did not wait till ufurped power had ftrengthened itfelf by exercife, and entangled the queftion in precedents. They faw all the confequences in the principle, and they avoided the confequences by denying the principle. We revere this leffon too much foon to forget it. Who does not fee that the fame authority which can eftablifh Chriftianity, in exclufion of all other religions,

(13)

ligions, may eftablifh, with the fame eafe, any particular fect of Chriftians, in exclufion of all other fects? That the fame authority which can force a citizen to contribute three pence only of his property for the fupport of any one eftablifhment, may force him to conform to any other eftablifhment, in all cafes whatfoever?

Becaufe, the bill violates that equality which ought to be the bafis of every law; and which is more indifpenfable, in proportion as the validity or expediency of any law is more liable to be impeached. If " all men are by nature equally free and independent," † all men are to be

† Declaration of Rights, Art. 1.

VI.4. "Who does not see," James Madison wrote in his *Memorial and Remonstrance* of 1786 against a bill to establish Christianity *in general* as the state religion, "that the same authority which can establish Christianity, in exclusion of all other Religions, may establish with the same ease any particular sect of Christians, in exclusion of all other sects?"

Thus, before he was fifty years old, Jefferson had witnessed the successful establishment of a new nation and the constitutional endorsement of the right to liberty of conscience in that nation. In his old age, reviewing a lifetime of extraordinary accomplishments, he asked to be remembered for only these: the founding of the University of Virginia, the writing of the Declaration of Independence, and his authorship of the Virginia statute establishing freedom of religion.

Thomas Jefferson was a deistic Episcopalian who was convinced that the apparent order of the universe demonstrated the existence of God to the rational mind without recourse to supernatural revelation. Serious differences in outlook separated a deist like Jefferson from the Baptist minister Isaac Backus or the radical seeker Roger Williams. But all three men were in agreement on one important point: belief cannot and should not be coerced; questions of faith ought to be decided between the individual and God. Although Williams had voiced this radical view over a century before Jefferson's or Backus's birth, liberty of conscience was still a novel idea in the late eighteenth century. The "lively experiment" that Rhode Islanders had taken up so many years before seemed an admirable and challenging one for the new nation to adopt in 1790, and the ideas of Williams and his companions were instituted on a much larger scale by the United States.

87

James Madison (1751–1836).
The Anti-Tyther: A Memorial and Remonstrance.
(Dublin, 1786)

Madison's *Memorial and Remonstrance* was composed in 1785 in opposition to "A Bill Establishing a Provision for Teachers of Christian Religion" that was being considered by the legislature. That bill was part of a movement to establish Christianity as the official religion, with freedoms granted only to those who professed it in some form. Under the provisions of the "Teacher's Bill" everyone would be taxed by the state toward the support of the Christian faith of their choice in a "general assessment." Rather than establishing one church and accepting certificates from certain dissenting sects, as was the practice in Connecticut and Massachusetts, this system would treat all accepted Christian faiths equally, requiring each person to support one of them. The Revolutionary leader Patrick Henry sponsored the bill, and many other patriots, including George Washington and Richard Henry Lee, hoped to see it pass. Madison, however, argued eloquently for complete liberty of conscience. After the Teacher's Bill was defeated, the way was open for the passage of Jefferson's Act guaranteeing religious freedom. The Dublin edition was published to convince the British Parliament to adopt similar policies (figure VI.4.).

88

The Bill of Rights, and Amendments to the Constitution of the United States, as Agreed to by the Convention of the State of Rhode-Island.
([Providence, 1790])

Rhode Island was the last state to ratify the Constitution. One of its objections to the document was that it lacked a bill of rights. The state convention considering the Constitution's ratification therefore drew up its own list of rights, which naturally included the right to religious liberty. Rhode Islanders were soon persuaded to join the union, in part by the passage of another such Bill of Rights by the first session of the Congress.

VI.5. Part of the entry on Shakers from Hannah Adams's *An Alphabetical Compendium of the Various Sects* (Boston, 1784).

89
Hannah Adams (1755–1831).
*An Alphabetical Compendium of the
Various Sects.*
(Boston, 1784)

The United Society of Believers in Christ's
Second Appearing, or Shakers, were one
of the many religious sects covered in
Hannah Adams's *Alphabetical Compen-*

dium. Adams, who never received any formal education due to her poor health, was
probably the first woman in America to
adopt writing as a career. That a Boston
press produced this objective treatment of
sectarianism is an indication of how far
that once intolerant town had come (figure
VI.5.).

90
Francis Asbury (1745–1816).
*An Extract from the Journal of Francis
Asbury, Bishop of the Methodist Episcopal
Church in America, From
August 7, 1771 to December 29, 1778.*
(Philadelphia, 1792)

When Methodism was established as a
separate denomination in England, the
church decided to send missionaries to the

American colonies. Asbury, son of a tenant
farmer and himself a blacksmith by training, was one of the first chosen. His *Journal*
recounted his efforts, and the growth of
Methodism during these early years. In
1784, he became the first bishop of the
Methodist church in America.

The religious diversity that had rendered freedom of choice so necessary to the
new nation increased during the Revolutionary era and beyond. Ann Lee, the
English founder of the new sect known as the Shakers, arrived in the colonies
just as the official break with England occurred. The Shakers were viewed with
suspicion at first, but were eventually accepted as the sincere religious group
they were. During the next century, Shaker communities sprang up all over the
United States. At its height in 1840 the sect had six thousand adherents living
in nineteen villages.

Methodism, which began as a Pietist movement within the Church of England, broke with that church to form a separate denomination in both England
and America during the 1780s. The Methodist Church grew to be one of the
largest Protestant denominations in the South, with congregations all over the
country.

King's Chapel, the Anglican church in Boston, became the first Unitarian
congregation in America after the rector and many of the Loyalist parishioners
fled during the Revolutionary War. The remaining members called the liberal
James Freeman to oversee their church, and in 1785 he introduced Unitarian
reforms. Early in the nineteenth century, this liberal religion would sweep
through New England, splitting many Congregational churches in two.

For those Anglicans who chose to remain in the United States after the
break with England, the Protestant Episcopal Church was created in 1789. This
new denomination maintained the practices and beliefs of the Church of England without the official connection to the English monarch as the head of that
church. In these four instances, the diversity that had long characterized the
British colonies increased unabated. As had always been the case, some new
faiths were imported, while others were created in the New World.

James Madison, perhaps the most able political theorist of the early American republic, frequently quoted the comment of the French philosopher Voltaire
explaining toleration in England in the eighteenth century:

If one religion were allowed in England, the Government would possibly
become arbitrary; if there were two, the people would cut each other's
throats; but as there are such a multitude, they all live happy and in peace.

yet neither are thofe innocent who lay them in their way;—that to fuffer the civil magiftrate to intrude his powers into the field of opinion, and to reftrain the profeffion or propagation of principles on a fuppofition of their ill tendency, is a dangerous fallacy, which at once deftroys all religious liberty; becaufe he, being of courfe judge of that tendency, will make his opinions the rule of judgment, and approve or condemn the fentiments of others, only as they fhall agree with or differ from his own; that it is time enough for the rightful purpofes of civil government, for its officers to inter-pofe, when principles break out in overt acts againft peace and good order;—and finally, that truth is great, and will prevail if left to herfelf; is the proper and fufficient antagonift to error; and can have nothing to fear from the conflict, unlefs (by human interpofition) difarmed of her natural weapons, free argument and debate; errors ceafing to be dangerous, when it is permitted freely to contradict them:

" Be it therefore enacted by the general affembly, that no man fhall be compelled to fupport any religious worfhip, place, or miniftry whatfoever; nor fhall be forced, reftrained, molefted or burthened in his body or goods, nor fhall otherwife fuffer, on account of his religious opinions or belief: but all men be free to profefs, and by argument to maintain, their opinion in matters of religion; and that the fame fhall in no wife diminifh, enlarge, or affect their civil capacities.

" And though we well know that this affembly, elected by the people for the ordinary purpofes of legiflation only, have no power to reftrain the acts of fucceeding affemblies, conftituted with powers equal to our own; and that therefore, to declare this act irre-vocable, would be of no effect in law; yet we are free to declare, and do declare, that the rights hereby afferted, are natural rights of mankind; and that if any act fhall be hereafter paffed to repeal the prefent, or to narrow its operation, fuch act will be no infringe-ment of natural rights."

ARTICLE XVIII.

A Parable againft Perfecution, by Dr. Franklin, *in Imitation of Scripture Language; founded upon a Jewifh Tradition* *.

AND it came to pafs after thefe things, that Abraham fat in the door of his tent, about the going down of the fun. And behold a man bent with age, coming from the way of the wildernefs leaning

* ' The following parable againft perfecution was communicated to me,' fays Lord
' Kairns, ' by Doctor Franklin, of Philadelphia, a man who makes a great figure in the
' lienated

leaning on a ftaff. And Abraham arofe and met him, and faid unto him, turn in I pray thee and wafh thy feet, and tarry all night; and thou fhalt arife early in the morning, and go on thy way. And the man faid, nay; for I will abide under this tree. But Abraham preffed him greatly: fo he turned and they went into the tent: and Abraham baked unleavened bread, and they did eat. And when Abraham faw that the man bleffed not God, he faid unto him, wherefore doft thou not worfhip the moft high God, creator of heaven and earth? And the man anfwered and faid, I do not worfhip thy God, neither do I call upon his name; for I have made to myfelf a God, which abideth always in my houfe, and providest me with all things. And Abraham's zeal was kindled againft the man, and he arofe, and fell upon him, and drove him forth with blows into the wildernefs. And God called unto Abraham, faying, Abraham, where is the ftranger? And Abraham anfwered and faid, Lord, he would not worfhip thee, neither would he call upon thy name; therefore have I driven him out from before my face into the wildernefs. And God faid, have I borne with him thefe hundred and ninety and eight years, and nourifhed him and clothed him, notwithftanding his rebellion againft me; and couldft not thou who art thyfelf a finner, bear with him one night?

Extracts from Obfervations on the Peopling of Countries, &c. By the fame.

THE great increafe of offspring in particular families is not always owing to greater fecundity of nature, but fometimes to examples of induftry in the heads, and induftrious education; by which the children are enabled to provide better for themfelves, and their marrying early is encouraged from the profpect of good fubfiftence. If there be a fect therefore, in our nation, that regard frugality and induftry as religious duties, and educate their children therein, more than others commonly do; fuch fect muft confe-quently increafe more by natural generation, than any other fect in Britain *.

' learned world; and who would ftill make a greater figure for benevolence and can-
' dour, were virtue as much regarded in this declining age as knowledge.
' ' The hiftorical ftyle of the Old Teftament is here finely imitated; and the moral muft
' ftrike every one who is not funk in ftupidity and fuperftition. Were it really a chapter
' of Genefis, one is apt to think, that perfecution could never have fhown a bare face
' among the Jews or Chriftians. But, alas! that is a vain thought. Such a paffage in
' the Old Teftament, would avail as little againft the rancorous paffions of men, as
' the follwing paffages in the New Teftament, though perfecution cannot be con-
' demned in terms more explicit. " He that is weak in the faith receive you, but not
' to doubtful difputations. For, &c."
* See another letter by Dr. Franklin on the fubject of religious liberty, in this collection, page 66.

N   ARTICLE

VI.6. One of a number of such testimonies by American Revolutionary leaders advocating religious toleration, this parable presented Franklin's views in a typically clever fashion. The parable appeared in an anthology published in London in 1790 entitled: *A Collection of Testimonies in favor of Religious Liberty.*

BENJAMIN FRANKLIN, LL.D. F.R.S.

VI.7. This portrait of Franklin, known as the "fur-capped Franklin," was immensely popular for its depiction of the great writer and statesman as a New World rustic. This engraving appeared in Washington Irving's *Life of George Washington* (New York, 1855).

91

A Collection of Testimonies in favor of Religious Liberty in the Case of the Dissenters, Catholics, and Jews, by a Christian Politician.
(London, 1790)

Political and social attitudes in Britain took a conservative turn in the 1790s as the French Revolution grew more and more violent. This pamphlet, compiled to combat this trend, cited the American example to prove that liberty did not always lead to

anarchy. The Virginia Assembly's "Act for Establishing Freedom of Religion" was reprinted, and such American luminaries as George Washington and Benjamin Franklin (figures VI.6. and 7.) were quoted. The example set by the new United States gave encouragement to European liberals for years to come and was often cited to bolster arguments in favor of religious equality and individual freedoms.

The British system that Voltaire so admired was one in which an established church existed, but various dissenting religious sects were tolerated. Such a system, although it was proving relatively successful in Britain, could not be adopted in the newly created United States. While one denomination might dominate numerically in a particular state, there was no likely candidate for a national established church. In addition, the fragile union of the states would not have survived any attempt by one group to impose its will on the others. The diversity that had long characterized the colonies precluded the British solution to the problem of what relationship the state ought to have to religion. In the United States the government would have to resign itself to accepting a multitude of beliefs and practices.

In the 1780s and 1790s, however, many of the nation's leaders may have been envisioning something much closer to the traditional system of limited toleration than the religious equality that Americans enjoy today. In 1783, when Ezra Stiles reveled in the new nation's religious diversity, he was thinking in terms of *Christian* sects being granted religious freedom. Modern Americans speak of the right to equal treatment for all beliefs, rather than the granting of liberty only to certain faiths.

Still, the groundwork was laid in these decades for the religious equality of the twentieth century. The Virginia "Act for Establishing Freedom of Religion" set the precedent of total state withdrawal from the regulation of religious practices, and the Bill of Rights prevented the federal government from intervening at all. After many years, much debate, and a great deal of social and political change, the principle of the complete separation of church and state has been generally accepted as one of the cardinal tenets of this nation. Liberty of conscience is probably one of the most frequently exercised of the rights guaranteed by the Bill of Rights.

The First Amendment strictures regarding religion are also among the most often debated Constitutional questions (figure VI.8.). In our own time, the Supreme Court has been called upon to decide such questions as the constitutionality of prayers in the public schools and the placement of crèches on public land at Christmastime. The underlying issue in these "church and state" cases is this: will any small breach in the neutrality of the state, any evidence of government favoritism of one religious practice over another, lead ultimately to some restriction of freedom? Complete freedom in religion, although generally accepted in principle, still requires working out in practice, as exemplified by the controversy surrounding the legitimacy of the Unification Church and the Reverend Moon. Two hundred years after the passage of Jefferson's "Act for Establishing Freedom of Religion in Virginia" and 350 years after Roger Williams launched his experiment in "soul liberty," liberty of conscience still has radical implications for our own society.

96

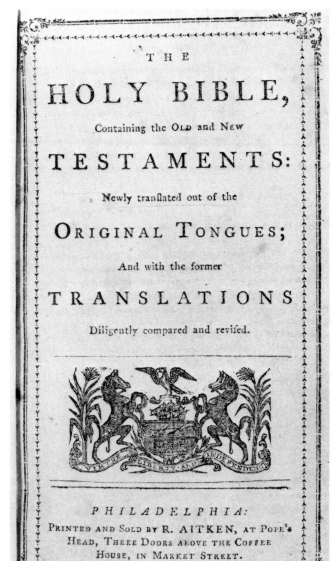

THE

HOLY BIBLE,

Containing the OLD and NEW

TESTAMENTS:

Newly translated out of the

ORIGINAL TONGUES;

And with the former

TRANSLATIONS

Diligently compared and revised.

VIRTUE LIBERTY AND INDEPENDENCE

PHILADELPHIA:

PRINTED AND SOLD BY R. AITKEN, AT POPE'S
HEAD, THREE DOORS ABOVE THE COFFEE
HOUSE, IN MARKET STREET.
M.DCC.LXXXII.

Whereupon,
RESOLVED,

THAT the United States in Congress assembled highly approve the pious and laudable undertaking of Mr. Aitken, as subservient to the interest of religion, as well as an instance of the progress of arts in this country, and being satisfied from the above report of his care and accuracy in the execution of the work, they recommend this edition of the Bible to the inhabitants of the United States, and hereby authorise him to publish this Recommendation in the manner he shall think proper.

CHA. THOMSON, Sec'ry.

VI.8. Robert Aitken's translation of the Bible, which appeared in 1782, was the first complete English edition published in America. The United States Congress, then meeting in Philadelphia, endorsed the work with a public resolution, the only such endorsement ever made by Congress. Before the decade was out, the ratification of the First Amendment of the Constitution would limit the government's freedom to make recommendations regarding religion.